LIFE
WITHOUT
LIMITS

ALSO BY
LUCINDA BASSETT

From Panic to Power

LIFE
WITHOUT
LIMITS

Conquer Your Fears,
Achieve Your Dreams,
and Make Yourself Happy

LUCINDA BASSETT

Quill
A HarperResource Book
An Imprint of HarperCollins*Publishers*

Quotations in chapters 8 through 11 are taken from *The Book of Positive Quotations,* compiled by John Cook, and reproduced by permission of the Fairview Press. Copyright Rubicon Press, 1993.

HarperCollins books may be purchased for educational, business, or sales promotional use. For information please write: Special Markets Department, HarperCollins Publishers Inc., 10 East 53rd Street, New York, NY 10022.

First HarperResource Quill paperback edition published 2002

Designed by Deborah Kerner

The Library of Congress has catalogued the hardcover edition as follows:

Bassett, Lucinda
    Life without limits : conquer your fears, achieve your dreams, and make yourself happy : a powerful book of self-discovery and transformation / Lucinda Bassett.
        p.   cm.
    ISBN 0-06-019658-0
    1. Success—Psychological aspects.   I. Title.

BF637.S8 B336 2001
158.1—dc21   00-064545

ISBN 0-06-095652-6 (pbk.)

02 03 04 05 06 ❖/RRD 10 9 8 7 6 5 4 3 2 1

THIS BOOK IS DEDICATED TO MY CHILDREN,

BRITTANY AND SAMMY,

AND MY HUSBAND, DAVID.

BEING YOUR MOTHER AND YOUR WIFE

AND SHARING OUR LIVES TOGETHER AS A FAMILY

HAS BEEN THE MOST INCREDIBLE GIFT GOD HAS GIVEN ME.

I AM A VERY LUCKY WOMAN.

HERE'S TO THE "DANCING BEARS" CLUB.

CONTENTS

ACKNOWLEDGMENTS

I would like to thank the wonderful friends and associates who have assisted me in bringing this book together. A very special thanks goes to my "wild and passionate" agent, Al (King) Lowman, for his belief in me. A very warm thank you goes to Diane Reverand, my editor at Cliff Street Books, for continuously believing in and supporting my message and my voice, and for her wonderful editing and insight. Thanks to Nansey Neiman-Legette for her editing assistance.

A special loving thank you to all my fellow worker bees at the Midwest Center: Carolyn, Barb, Larry, Monica, Jim, Darla, Kathy, Lisa, Jenny, and Dawn. If it weren't for all of you doing all the things you do so well, I wouldn't have the time to write books.

A special loving thank you to my mother for giving me a sense of myself, my potential, and a clear understanding of what really matters in life. Thank you for your pride in me; it is such a motivating force. By the way, the feeling is mutual.

A loving thank you to my brother Michael for helping to shine the light of the Midwest Center through his incredible production talents. And a loving thank you to my big brother Gary for believing in me and loving me so unconditionally.

And finally, a special warm hug and thank you to David, my husband of 18 years and partner in life. You truly are the wind beneath my wings. I love you.

INTRODUCTION

Opportunities are everywhere. Contrary to public opinion, opportunity knocks more than once. The truth is, it will knock again and again, until it literally knocks you over. That's because opportunity is not a random event; it arises as a direct result of circumstance and attitude. When you know exactly what you want, when you believe in yourself, and when you have a plan of action, the potential for opportunity and success on every level of your life becomes limitless. Anything is possible.

Success has been described as the moment when preparation meets opportunity. This book is about being completely prepared and confident for the moment when the opportunities you create open themselves up to you. This book is about defining what you want and then using all of your skills to get it by following the path of least resistance.

Success is a relative term that can be defined in various ways. To some, success is all about money: acquiring it, controlling it, having enough to last a lifetime. To others, the appeal of being financially successful is really the appeal of having the freedom to live their lives the way they want. Many people want money because they enjoy the "things" money can buy—houses, cars, and other material possessions. For someone who is struggling with illness or loss, living successfully becomes less about money and more about health and well-being. Simply stated, success encompasses affluence, abundance, happiness, and well-being. In this book, we will be looking closely at various levels of success and satisfaction their elusiveness, and their acquisition.

For many people, acquiring and maintaining wealth, abundance, happiness, and success on any level is difficult if not impossible because worry, uncertainty, and fear also knock more than once. In fact, insecurity can and probably will arise whenever you reach for a goal. If you see yourself as someone who isn't smart enough, strong enough, or confident enough, if you worry about being too old, too uneducated, or simply incapable, insecurity is the face you'll be reflecting to the world. You will become an expert at justifying your inability to make your dreams a reality.

Our perception of ourselves begins when we're children. Have you ever heard a group of kindergartners talking about what they want to be when they grow up? They wiggle with enthusiasm and excitement as they rattle off their ever-changing list. They believe they can be anything from movie stars to astronauts, so they never consider that reaching their goals may not be possible. Their nature is to believe that they can do anything they choose.

It's safe to say that we are born dreamers. As we grow older, the time we used to spend dreaming of unlimited possibilities becomes time we devote to worrying. In fact, we get so good at being negative and self-defeating that we become our own worst enemies. All too soon, we're wasting time agonizing over past periods in our lives when we would have, should have, and could have. Exposure to other people's ideas and attitudes and, in many cases, a lack of positive input can make us insecure.

And then we wonder where the years went and why we aren't fulfilled.

Unfortunately, the majority of us didn't get supportive messages when we were growing up. In fact, most of us got the opposite. We were told that life is tough and dreams don't often come true. We were told, or it was implied, that we should do what is sensible and predictable instead of pursuing a dream that might challenge us. For the few of us who did get positive messages, we lost them somewhere along the way, or we were negatively influenced by other people's fears or by the rest of the world around us. These influences led us to engage in unhealthy comparisons and to question our own abilities.

That's when we started second-guessing ourselves, wondering if maybe we really weren't good enough, smart enough, attractive enough, or talented enough to make it. Perhaps this is what systematically breaks us down until we decide to surrender by taking what we consider to be the easiest, most attainable path. Then, for no apparent reason, we end up frustrated with ourselves and how our lives are going. What we thought was the path of least resistance, the easy way out, is really the path of "most resistance." Instead of our decisions bringing us peace and satisfaction, we find discontent gnawing at our insides and have the sense that we are somehow in the wrong place, with the wrong people, doing the wrong things. Satisfaction seems to elude us.

Since I founded the Midwest Center for Stress and Anxiety in 1985, I've had the opportunity to work with hundreds of thousands of people. During my various lectures and seminars in cities across the country, whether I was addressing corporations, independent professionals, or local community groups or working with individuals, I would ask the same question: "If I could tap you on the head with a magic wand and you could have, do, and be anything you wanted right now, what would you ask for?" I was surprised and saddened to discover that eight out of ten people were dumbfounded. They just stared at me, unable to answer this simple question. It became obvious to me that far too many people share a common experience: their dreams have died. The death of their dreams is accompanied by, if not the result of, a lack of clarity about what they want and how to get it.

What do you see when you look in the mirror? A self-confident, radiant, intuitive person who is living life to the fullest? Or do you see a frustrated, insecure, fearful person with the inability to make good decisions? When the magic wand taps you on the head, do you know how to get what you want? Do you even know what you want?

In all my travels, I am continually amazed at the number of people who are personally, professionally, and financially frustrated. The worst part is that they don't really know why. If they could change things, they aren't sure how or even what they would change. It becomes painfully clear that many people never defined their dreams way back when they began their journey. This certainly was the case for me.

In retrospect, I spent a good part of my life drifting. I worked hard, but I didn't have any direction. I didn't know what I was working for or toward. It was frustrating and unfulfilling; but due to lack of clarity and confidence, I just kept going. I wasn't happy, satisfied, committed, or passionate about anything. I knew I wanted something, I knew something was missing, but I couldn't define it.

As fate would have it, chronic fear and severe anxiety disorder, probably manifested partially as a result of my sense of drift, led me to do some serious soul searching. I had to look closely inside myself and to get clear about the life I wanted to live and what I wanted for myself. I knew if I didn't, I would stay stuck. I looked my fears in the face, defused my demons, and started to define my desires clearly and specifically. Could it be it wasn't too late? Did I still have a chance to fulfill a dream? Could I even define the dream? And, was I really capable of making it my reality? I began to step out of my comfort zone. I began to ask myself what mattered to *me*. I began to believe in myself. I made different choices for reasons that finally made sense. I started to focus on what I wanted instead of on what I was afraid of. I started to take major risks, and I got addicted to the excitement of challenging myself. I was fully alive and confident for the first time in my life. I gave myself permission to fail, to be embarrassed, and to make mistakes. Just as important, I gave myself permission to be successful and happy. This new behavior, this new way of thinking, *dramatically* changed my life.

I went from perceiving myself as a poor little girl from an alcoholic parent, who grew up in a brown-shingled house at the end of a dead-end street, someone who wasn't worthy or special, to seeing myself as someone who could change herself, and maybe even change the world.

Way back when I was second-guessing myself and struggling with severe anxiety, I never would have dreamed such incredible success could have come my way. Once I changed my attitude, I changed my life.

Not all of us want to write books or have our own business; but the point is, if I can make my dreams a reality, so can you. I don't know about you, but when I learn something from someone, I want to learn it from someone who has lived it and made it happen in his or her own life. You can't really give good advice on how to build a multi-million-dollar company unless you've done it. You can't help someone else overcome a problem with anxiety unless you've conquered your own fears. You certainly can't teach someone how to achieve a satisfying life unless you have one. I have learned how to do these things in my life, and it is an honor and a divinely driven desire for me to share these skills with you.

The beautiful thing is that we are all capable of achieving a satisfying, fulfilling life. We can all get to wherever it is we want to go. We just need clarity, motivation, and really good directions.

So how about you? Have you clearly defined what you want for yourself? Do you think about becoming more secure or independently wealthy? Would you like to open your own business? Or write a book? Do you imagine going to college or owning a cabin by a lake? Do you fantasize about getting married to the love of your life and raising a family? Would you like to lose weight or be more confident? Would you like to be an artist, a motivational speaker, or a stand-up comic? Possibly you'd like to be a better parent or have a more loving and supportive relationship. Maybe you just want to have more fun and more friends. Or possibly you want a sense of direction; you want to feel satisfied and have more peace of mind. Maybe you'd just like to know what you want for a change.

The good news is that it's not too late. What if someone handed you a guaranteed road map to successful living, one that absolutely works?

This book is that road map. It is the complete guide to attaining abundance in every area of your life. It begins by showing you how to change your perception of the meaning of success. It will show you how to change your perception of the person you see in the mirror by getting back in touch with your belief in yourself and with your ability to determine your own destiny. You will begin to dream again and to define those dreams clearly and with passion. Then you will transform your fear, worry, and negative ideas about yourself into positive, confident, creative energy that you didn't even know you had. You'll learn to trust yourself and your decisions, and you'll become skilled at taking calculated risks.

In this book, you will participate in specific personal assessments that will show you where your frustration is coming from. You'll learn specific skills to help you get out there and make things happen in your life, right now. You'll also learn how to recognize divine clues and how to activate your intuitive power to help you clarify and achieve your dreams.

The bottom line is this: it's time to stop worrying, stop procrastinating, and stop making excuses. It's time to make positive new changes in your life. If you've forgotten how to dream and you don't know what you want, you can't possibly be motivated and enthusiastic. It's hard to be happy or successful when you have no sense of direction. How can you pursue something that you can't define?

When you're clear about what success means for you, when you clarify your dreams and start doing what you want, you will begin to recognize the presence of universal and personal power in your life. Synchronicity arises, and the desired events of your life start unfolding. Providence comes into play, because you are doing what you love and following your heart. Opportunities will present themselves, new doors will open, and, to your amazement, all sorts of wonderful things will begin to happen.

Until one is committed, there is hesitancy,
the chance to draw back, always ineffectiveness.
Concerning all acts of initiative (and creation)
there is one elementary truth, the ignorance
of which kills countless ideas and splendid plans:
that the moment one definitely commits oneself,
then Providence moves, too.
All sorts of things occur to help one that would never
otherwise have occurred.
A whole stream of events issues from the decision,
raising in one's favor all manner of unforeseen incidents
and meetings and material assistance,
which no man could have dreamed
would have come his way.

—W. H. MURRAY

Part I

YOU HAVE
TO KNOW
WHAT
YOU WANT
BEFORE YOU
CAN GET IT

1

REDEFINING SUCCESS

Happiness is to be found along the way, not at the end of the road, for then the journey is over and it is too late. Today, this hour, this minute is the day, the hour, the minute for each of us to sense the fact that life is good, with all of its trials and troubles, and perhaps more interesting because of them.

— R O B E R T   U P D E G R A F T

What Is Success?

Think about your life exactly as it is, and do an honest evaluation. Are you happy with the way your life is going right now? Do you like the way you live? Do you get up feeling excited about the day and grateful to be in your experience? Are you happy with the way you look and the way you feel physically? Are you confident? Do you like who you are? Are you financially and professionally satisfied? What about your daily experiences—do you like the places you go, the way you spend your time, and the people with whom you spend time? How do you feel about yourself and your life before you go to sleep at night? And finally, have you ever sincerely asked yourself these questions, or is it a brand new experience to be examining your life to this degree?

Think about people in your life or people you have met whom you really admire, possibly even envy. What about them impresses you? Is it their lifestyle or their spiritual convictions? Is it their ability to make and keep good friends? Are you envious of their career, the things they have, or the money they spend? Possibly someone you know and admire seems content and happy most of the time, and you wonder why you can't feel this way.

You may know someone who seems to have a good marriage and to truly love and enjoy his or her spouse, a form of personal success you may not have been able to achieve. Maybe you know someone who really enjoys his or her family, but you find yours to be a source of disappointment and irritation. Do you watch in amazement as a friend enjoys her job, while you toil away feeling professionally frustrated and unhappy? Do you know someone who keeps himself healthy, eating well, exercising, and taking care of his body, while you struggle to wake up with your morning coffee and desperately anticipate that evening drink to relax? Does someone you know seem easy going, able to handle crisis and stress, while you secretly struggle with the guilt of your consistent irritability and your feelings of being overwhelmed?

Success Is a Relative Concept

As you can see, there are various types of successful living, and they are different for everyone. Success is a relative concept. For many of us, being successful means living a healthy, long life, contented with friends and family. For others, it means doing what we love and looking forward to the daily experience of doing it. Still others define success as achieving lifelong dreams and ambitions, working toward something they are passionate about. The acquisition of material possessions would be success for some people. And I am certain success for many would be defined as having lots of money and total financial security. Even that is relative, depending on the lifestyle you desire.

> *"I don't make deals for the money. I've got enough, much more than I'll ever need. I do it to do it. Other people paint beautifully on canvas or write wonderful poetry. I like making deals, preferably big deals. That's how I get my kicks."*
>
> —DONALD TRUMP

When you look at people who are perceived as being very successful, the Rupert Murdochs, the Donald Trumps, and the Bill Gateses of the world, you might think that success is all about acquiring great wealth. In a recent interview, Donald Trump, when asked what made him so ambitious, said nothing about money. In fact, he said that it's the challenge and the love of competition that drives him. He probably has more money now than he'd ever be able to spend, and yet he still keeps wheeling and dealing. Why? Trump loves what he does, and he is passionate about it. Acquiring great wealth was a by-product of following his passion to build an empire that would provide him with the opportunity to do what he loves, play the game.

I read a magazine article a few years ago about Stephen King, the fabulously creative writer of so many horror novels and movies with which we're all familiar. He is a very wealthy man, yet he chooses to live in a simple Victorian house in his hometown. His kids go to the local school, and attend the local church. His office is a small little room in the back of an old factory. He used his money to build a new baseball field for the community schools. Obviously his success isn't about being wealthy, about riding in limousines and flashing expensive jewelry. In fact, the article made clear that all King wanted to do was write and live a "simple" life. Finding success was a long, hard journey for Stephen King. He worked in a laundromat for years and wrote in his spare time. He was tempted at times to throw his work away, frustrated that it wasn't getting recognition from publishers. After years of determination and stick-to-itiveness, he achieved his dream of become a best-selling author. Wealth was never his motivation. Being able to write and to make a living at it, and having his work acknowledged, was success for King.

Our Definition of Success
Changes Throughout Our Lives

So what exactly is *success*, and does its definition vary depending on the definer's age, marital status, upbringing, and expectations?

When we are teenagers, success probably means doing well in school and being socially accepted. As we move into our early twenties, we start to think about our identity and what type of future we want for ourselves. At this time, many of us look for a sense of direction, a long-term relationship, and something we can feel passionate about on a personal level. Personally, I didn't have a clue about what I really wanted back then. I just knew I wanted to see the world and enjoy myself.

By the time many of us are in our middle to late twenties and early thirties, we are going in a direction professionally that was neither planned nor anticipated. Some of us end up working very hard, because this is a passionate age, but we are sometimes working at jobs that we aren't all that passionate about. Often, we start looking outside ourselves for fulfillment. We wonder what's missing, what *we* are missing. If we are in a relationship, sometimes they end; if we aren't committed, sometimes we become so, often in search of stimulation.

This is often the time many people have children, which in itself can be a distraction from finding and satisfying our inner calling. Parenting, although rewarding, is totally consuming. There isn't much time for reflection on our lives as individuals. During this time, most people get caught up in the frenzy of attempting to juggle their children's lives and schedules with their own. Parents, especially mothers, often end up making personal and professional choices based on the needs of the children.

By the time we are in our forties, we're looking around saying to ourselves, am I fulfilled? Did I get and do I have the life I want? Sadly for many people, if they haven't taken a serious look at themselves, they reach fifty and say, "Wait a minute. Who am I, and what have I become? Am I even happy? My life is half over, and I'm not sure I feel good about myself, where I am in my life, and what I've accomplished."

Define Your Dreams,
Determine Your Future

When we get to our fifties and wonder where we are, what we fail to realize is that we forgot one important step along the way. We forgot to define what we wanted when we started the process of working passionately. Can you imagine how your life might be different if you had had clear vision back in your twenties—if you would have known exactly what you wanted, right down to the last detail, and you had a clear plan of action as to how to get it? Wouldn't it be great if this were something they taught us in high school along with math and English?

Think back for a moment. Would you have made different decisions along the way? Would you be somewhere completely different in your life from where you are now? If you had had a clear vision about what you wanted for yourself, you would have made decisions based on what you wanted and what you didn't want. Decision making would have been much easier. You might be thinking that it's hard to know what you want at seventeen. This may be true, but why are so many people still lost and frustrated at thirty-five and fifty?

I know a brilliant woman with an MBA from a prestigious school. In her late forties, she is professionally successful. Recently, she came to me with severe anxiety and sleeping problems. She was living in Chicago, making a great deal of money working in sales and syndication for a major newspaper, and yet she was depressed and anxious. In our sessions, we soon discovered the reason for many of her problems. She was personally frustrated, and she was dissatisfied with her chosen career. In our conversations, she said she never really wanted to go into this type of business. She always loved working with kids. She secretly wanted to be a teacher and live a simpler life. She was sick of the hustle and bustle and the pressure of her job, and she wanted a different lifestyle.

She felt as if she had followed in her father's footsteps, and as a result, she was very financially successful. But she was so busy that she never really gave herself time for marriage and children. She had regrets. She was lonely, tired, and sad. It was obvious she wasn't living the life she really wanted. Unfortunately, she was just getting down to the business of figuring it out. I convinced her that it wasn't too late to go after her dreams, now that she had clearly defined them. She could still get married and even bring children into her life, if that's what she really wanted. She certainly could be a wonderful teacher. The good news is that the money she had made could allow her the freedom to take some chances.

Frustration and dissatisfaction can happen at different ages, and it doesn't always happen the same way for everyone. It also happens to people who are considered successful, even wealthy. It's called "losing sight of our dreams somewhere along the way." It's called "selling out for what seemed to make sense at the time." Often we'll spend years spinning our wheels, running as fast as we can, never stopping to look at whether we like where we are or are even happy.

Success is a state we can achieve at any time in our lives. It is a place in which a person is enjoying his life experience. Successful living is when you are in loving relationships, have good friends, and are somewhat financially comfortable. Success is having a sense of contentment with what you are doing, a sense of peace about where and who you are, no matter where you are in your life, and a sense of purpose that you are working toward something about which you are passionate. I also believe good health to be a form of success, but I know many people who are living remarkably successful lives who aren't healthy because they are challenged with a life-threatening or debilitating chronic disease.

Is success something you have to be a certain age to achieve? Not necessarily. Young children and aging adults can experience success on many levels. Is it something you only experience if you are wealthy? Certainly not. In fact, some wealthy people I know have never achieved many of the things I've mentioned here. Does success of this type come with a price tag? Yes, self-evaluation, clarity, and effort. Does your concept of success change throughout your life? Absolutely. By clarifying what you want early on, you are more likely not to waste time on what you don't want or, even more important, not to end up in the wrong place.

You are full of ideas, dreams, desires, and feelings. Your mind is a powerful tool that offers you incredible information if you just pay attention. You have specific talents and skills that make you perfect for something, if you only knew what it was! It isn't easy to define it at nineteen, and for some, it isn't any easier to do at forty-five.

My definition of success for myself has changed over the years. If you would have asked me in my twenties what success meant to me and for me, I would have said something totally different from what I would say now in my forties. When I was in my twenties, in retrospect, and with a bit of embarrassment, I think I would have said success to me was a career as a famous singer/entertainer; a tall, dark, handsome, and wealthy husband; a home in some beautiful tropical place on the water; and traveling the world. Did the things I wanted in my twenties become my reality? No. That was my fantasy life, the one I dreamed about, particularly on frustrated days.

I didn't really define my desires realistically, and I certainly didn't form a plan of action to get them. I know now that if that was what I had really wanted, and if I would have focused on it and worked to make it happen, I could have had my fantasy life, right down to the wealthy husband. But then, I thought: *I come from a poor family, my father was a car salesman. What wealthy, sophisticated guy would want me?* I didn't see myself then as an attractive, intelligent woman who could interest a sophisticated man. *I am a good singer*, I thought to myself, *but I don't sing as well as Barbra Streisand, so why bother trying to make it?* I didn't know that "making it" as a singer wasn't as much about talent as it was about stick-to-itiveness and determination. I stopped myself by undercutting myself with success sabotage attitudes (something we will discuss later in the book). More than a few times in my life, my gut instinct was to go for it as an entertainer, but I didn't know anything about listening to my intuition back then. I only did what I was programmed to do after years of practice. I gave myself all the reasons why I could never make it. They worked.

As the years unfolded in my life, I went through many frustrating self-evaluation experiences. I had some great excuses for why I wasn't living the life I wanted to live. I wasn't talented enough or pretty enough. And, of course, my father was an alcoholic, so no wonder I was so insecure and unworthy. I even had a problem with severe anxiety and panic attacks, which I think I created as another excuse not to pursue my dreams. What if I couldn't handle it? I'd better just stay where it was safe and familiar—another sabotage syndrome.

I ended up in media sales, and I did well financially. I did some creative work in television and radio, but as a result of my lack of clarity and my constant self-sabotage, I didn't stick to anything. I continued to drift. I knew I wasn't satisfied, but I didn't have any sense of direction. I was thirty, time was ticking by, and I was feeling unhappy and unfulfilled. Finally, when I started dealing with my severe anxiety, I was forced to take a long, hard look at myself. It boiled down to this: Did I want to continue being miserable and frustrated and blaming everyone and everything around me for my unhappiness? Or did I want to step up to the plate, take responsibility, and change my life and probably my future?

When I began to evaluate my definition of happiness and success for myself, I figured out that what I really wanted was a loving supportive partner, children, a career that enabled me to make a difference in the world, and an opportunity to use my "entertainer" personality. I also decided I did want to live by the water!

Now at forty-three, I would define success as good health for myself and my family, plenty of time to be there for my family (especially my children), a sense of peace about my life, feeling good about who I am and where I'm going, lots of free time to spend doing things I want to do, great vacations (I love vacations), helping people empower themselves, and writing books that inspire people. Because I know what I want, I now make decisions that will help me get there and stay there. Because I am so very clear about what I want for my daily life experience, I simply say no to things that won't get me there and yes to things that will.

I sometimes wonder where I would be in my life now if I had known back in my twenties what I know now: You can do and be anything you want if you just figure out what it is and stay determined and focused. Would I have moved to New York and made it as a singer? Who knows? I only know that I am glad I figured out what I wanted in my early thirties, because I like what I've become.

I wonder where I would be now if I had not figured it out. Would I still be struggling and frustrated? Would I be working at a job I hate? Would I be divorced a few times and possibly not even be a mother? Would I not be living by the ocean and enjoying my daily life experience so fully? Who knows what bad decisions I might have made in the name of frustration and personal dissatisfaction.

Do You Know What Success Means to You?

If you define what success means, you may just find that your definition of success and what you want for yourself on long-term and on daily bases are very different. In fact you may find that what you think you want and what would make you *happy* are two different things. You might even find that what you think would make you feel successful could have a negative impact on your daily living experience. For example, if I did become a prominent entertainer, it could take away from my daily experience of being with my children. I would have to make a decision about which was more important to me and what was my true definition of success.

You might even find with careful evaluation that what you have right now is what you really want and that is why it exists for you. This finding can be quite a relief because it allows you to create a new goal that will provide a secondary fulfillment that you might be missing. If you find that what you want isn't in your reality, it is time to take control and figure out how to make it happen.

In your quest for success, it is extremely important that you define success for *yourself*. How else how can you possibly know otherwise when you've achieved it? How can you possibly devise a plan of action to make it happen if you are unclear about what success means for you?

When people believe they are dying, they tend to naturally pursue whatever it is they think they still need to experience or do. If they were content with how their life experience was going before they got sick, they just tend to want to appreciate what they have. If they weren't satisfied with how they were living life before their illness, they sometimes do unusual things.

I remember a very special woman who was diagnosed several years ago with a rare, terminal disease. She was strong, smart, and independent. She was in her late thirties, married, with no children. She was raised in a very money-conscious family. Even though they were quite comfortable financially, her parents always purchased used cars and lived in simple, moderately furnished homes. When Sharon grew up, she herself became hugely successful in sales, at times making upward of $20,000 a month. Yet she, too, bought used cars and lived a simple life.

She would shop at bargain stores and always hit the sale racks. Something changed in the last several months of her life when she knew she was dying. I went to visit her and was amazed to find she had purchased a brand new sports car . . . in red. During my visit, she wanted to go shopping, and, boy, did she shop! She bought expensive clothing and expensive shoes, and I was even surprised to find that she was redoing her kitchen in a very upscale fashion.

We never discussed her change in behavior. I was glad she was enjoying herself. She got so much pleasure from driving around in that car. When she passed away, I found myself wondering why she hadn't purchased it years before, why she hadn't spent some of the money she had on the things she wanted when she was healthy and could have really enjoyed them? She certainly had it to spend and then some. She was professionally successful, but it was obvious she never gave herself permission to have the things in life she wanted even though she could easily afford them. Did she not know she wanted these things? Did she not know how much pleasure having them would add to her daily experience? It made me sad to think that she could have been enjoying the feeling of riding around in that car years ago.

Another woman I know who was diagnosed with an incurable, life-threatening disease also did something surprising to me. On hearing that she had less than five years to live, she drastically changed her personal life. She left her husband of twenty years and started going out dancing and dating. She told me that they never really had what she considered a healthy, loving relationship. She said that she wanted to experience real love and passion and that if she only had a short time to live, she was going to find it somehow. At a time when you think she would have felt vulnerable and afraid, wanting to cling to her familiar surroundings and support system, she took a major chance. She did find a new, very gentle, loving man, who fell in love with her in spite of the diagnosis. I am happy to say she is still alive today—twelve years later!

Is what she did right or wrong? It doesn't matter to anyone but her. It is her journey. It was her quest for a fulfilling life. For her, it meant finding true love before it was too late. Was Sharon wrong to buy an expensive car and expensive things before she died? Of course not; again it is her wants and desires that determine what is right for her. There's nothing wrong with wanting and enjoying nice things. The sad truth is that they could have both been living the life they wanted years before, if only they had been honest with themselves about what they really wanted and had given themselves permission to have it.

If you knew you were dying, what do you think you would want more of, money or time? Of course, you would want more time. If you had an illness that was going to cut your life short, but you didn't know for certain how short, how would you want to spend your remaining time? How would you want to spend your days if you knew you maybe had two to five years left? I say two to five years instead of six months, because you would respond completely differently if you only had a few months. If you only had a few months, you might spend it saying good-bye or taking care of business. If you had a few years, your choices would be about enjoying your life. What would you do differently if you only had two to five years left? Would you live somewhere different? Would you work less and play more? Would you spend more time with certain people and less with others? This is one way to begin asking yourself what a successful daily life experience means for you.

You don't want to spend a lifetime being uncertain or falling short of your desires. You don't have to wait until something dramatic happens to realize you haven't been living the life you want to live. You just need to do a personal assessment of what it is you do want and then devise a plan of action to make it happen.

The point is that your daily life experience is a choice you make. You have to know what you really want, how you want to spend your time, and what is really important to you.

Variations on Successful Living

So what are some of the different types of successful lives that people have chosen for themselves? Here are some examples of successful living that I have been fortunate enough to observe or hear about:

One of the most successful people I've ever met has very little money. She is someone I have envied at times. She lives in a log cabin in a small midwestern town. She is beautiful in a very natural way, intelligent, and incredibly aware of herself. She grows her own vegetables, owns a few horses, and loves opera. At any given time and on any given day, she is teaching something either to herself or to someone lucky enough to spend time with her. She was a born teacher and spiritual guide. She doesn't have a lot of money, but then she doesn't need a lot of money for the lifestyle she's chosen. As simple as her lifestyle is, she has a more successful life than many wealthy people I know. She is living the life she wants to live the way she wants to live it—riding her horses, eating wonderful food from her garden, being surrounded by a healthful, earthy environment, and sharing her time with interesting, intelligent people who are on a similar spiritual path.

On the opposite end of the spectrum, I know a man in his fifties named Chuck, who started a small manufacturing company twenty years ago. He was happily building his company and his security over the years, but then, at the suggestion of his accountant and banker, he decided to take his company public. In the past few years, his newfound wealth has astounded even him. He now owns homes in southern California, Hawaii, and New York. He has a private jet and travels back and forth from New York to Los Angeles. He's a loving family man, loves his business, and is having the time of his life traveling the world. He was happy before the money, but the newfound wealth has generated fun for him and his family.

My brother Gary worked hard for many years, raised his family, and decided it was time to realize his dream. He has always wanted to live in the Florida Keys. In addition, he has been a musician all his life, but he didn't have the time to really pursue it professionally. He moved to the Keys and got a job on weekends singing and playing music. He bought a boat and a small house on the water. Now, he spends his days the way he always dreamed of living them. He usually spends his afternoons fishing, cruising on his boat, or working around his yard. His evenings are spent enjoying the balmy Florida breezes and beautiful sunsets. On the weekends he is entertaining people with his music and his jokes. Just recently Mom and I went to visit him. He had a beard, he was trim, and tanned, and he was happy as a clam. How many of us dream of doing something like this but are too afraid to go after it?

Recently, I had the pleasure of meeting an interesting character who actually lived in a neighborhood in California near Johnny Carson most of her life. This eccentric older woman named Meredith was married to a very wealthy movie producer at one time. They built a beautiful mansion on a cliff looking out at the ocean. They raised a family, partied with the likes of Elizabeth Taylor and Shirley MacLaine, and lived a life many would think enviable. One day a few years ago, her husband came home and announced that he was in love with another woman. Needless to say, Meredith was devastated at first. Once he left, she realized many things about herself. For one thing, she hated the mansion and decided she would move to a cozy house in the mountains. She also realized that she wanted to climb mountains. She began trekking in places like Kathmandu and Tibet. She started painting and has even had her work featured in art galleries. She told me she has never been happier or more at peace. She was so busy living the life her former husband wanted to live that she didn't even bother to think about what would make her truly happy.

The other day I asked a physician colleague of mine whom he considered successful. He told me a story about a man in his hometown who owned the local hardware store. My colleague had always been enamored of this man's seemingly contented life. He had four kids, and lived a very simple life in a small home. He ran the store, was on a first name basis with everyone in town, and was very active in the community. He always seemed happy and in a pleasant mood. My colleague said he has thought about that man occasionally throughout his own life as a way of reminding himself how important the simple pleasures in life are.

I think of success and what it means to my little boy, Sammy, who struggles with fine motor delay and Tourette's syndrome. He works ten times harder than other seven-year-olds just to write a simple, four-letter word. Not long ago, he took his first second-grade spelling test, which consisted of various difficult sentences, long words, and the use of quotations. He struggled to do his homework and study for this test, all the while anticipating his inability to perform well and in a timely fashion. "Mommy," he cried on the final night before the test, "I'll never be able to do it. I can't write as fast as the other kids. I'll fail." I told him, "Sammy, you're smart and you have a great memory. Just focus on what you're doing, take the time you need, and don't worry about how neat it is. Trust yourself. You have studied hard. You know the words and you will do just fine." I knew he was as prepared as he could be. I'll never forget the look on his face when I picked him up from school the day of his test. He was sitting outside the room on a picnic table waiting for me. His papers were spread out on the table with the spelling test strategically placed on top. He looked up at me, grinned, and looked away out of shy pride. There on the top of the pile of papers was a perfect test! He was so proud. That was success for Sammy.

Success Starts on the Inside

Is success always about the simple things in life? Of course not. Is it wrong to want expensive things or to desire great wealth, and is it wrong to equate success with having them? No. But I believe it is very difficult to find pleasure from things or money if you aren't happy with yourself to begin with. If you are a frustrated, unhappy person, no amount of material possessions or money will make you happy.

Figure out what you want from life, how you want to live, how you want to spend your time. If having more materialistically or financially is part of it, give yourself permission to have it. Form a plan of action to get what you want on every level. The ultimate goal is to be happy with who you are in your present moment, to make plans and have dreams, to know what you want and where you are going. Then everything you bring into your life experience will be a wonderful addition to an *already* successful life.

I like to divide success into three primary categories:

> *Personal success is achieved*
> *when you feel good about*
> *yourself and your relationships*

- You feel good about yourself physically—the way you feel and look, your weight, your energy, your health, and the way you take care of yourself.
- You have good friendships and healthy personal relationships.
- You have a good support system, interesting uplifting people with whom to spend time, and time to spend with these people.
- You have a sense of family and know they are available to you.
- You feel good about yourself as a parent if you are a parent.
- You feel good about your marriage or partnership.
- You feel good spiritually.
- You have a sense of integrity about who you are.
- You know what is important to you, what you want for yourself.

- You live the way you want to live and spend your time doing things you want to do.

Professional Success

Career satisfaction means having a sense of professional achievement:

- You are stimulated by what you do; you have drive and ambition, motivation, and a feeling of excitement about your career.
- You are happy with your chosen field; you know where you are going and what your long-term goals are.
- You feel excited to go to work and to do your work.
- You feel good about the work you do, and you are proud to talk about it.
- You have a strong sense that what you do matters, that your work is good and valuable.
- You feel that you are valuable.

Financial Success

Financial success is relative, so it is important to consider the following questions:

- How much money do you need in order to feel financially successful?
- What kind of house do you want to live in? Where?
- What kind of car do you want to drive?
- How often do you want to go out to eat? How often do you want to take vacations?

- What kind of spending money do you need weekly? Monthly?
- How do you want to dress and present yourself to the world?
- How much do you need to live the life you want right now, in the future, and for retirement?
- How much money do you need to have to feel financially secure?

Being able to provide for yourself the way you want and not feel insecure or pressured, being able to enjoy spending some of your money comfortably now and still put a nice sum of money away for the future, this is true financial success.

In reading through the definitions of personal, professional, and financial success, do you see areas where you need improvement? Do you feel successful in one area but not in another? Which areas need the most clarification and intervention? We will be spending a great deal of time with these categories in the next few chapters.

When you begin to clarify what you want, you may discover that it isn't that far away or that difficult to achieve. Or possibly what you think success is and what you really want for yourself and your daily life experience are quite different.

To benefit from this book, I think it would be very helpful at this time for you to begin a journal. Several of the chapters in this book end with questions for personal evaluation and introspection. Try to think about the questions, and explore them fully in your mind. I suggest you write the answers in your journal so you can keep track of your thoughts and do some serious self-assessment.

Let's Examine What Success Is For You Now

What is success? Take a few minutes to think about this. First write down what success is, generally speaking. Then write down what it would mean for you personally.

In your opinion, how does the world and how do other people define success?

Does it matter to you that you fit that profile, to appear successful to the outside world?

What successful people do you know, and why are they successful? What is it about them that would you like to emulate?

What does success bring to a person (e.g., respect, opportunity, more free time)?

What does success do for a person psychologically? Does it give a person, for example, greater sense of self-esteem, more social acceptance, more independence?

What do successful people look like? Do they dress differently? Do they carry themselves differently?

Who in your immediate family is successful and in what way? How has this affected other family members? You?

In what areas of your life have you been successful—career? relationships? How does it feel to be successful?

In what areas of your life would you like to be more success-ful—career? relationships? personal issues?

What dream or dreams would you like to fulfill? What is hold-ing you back? Could it be fear or insecurity, lack of direction, lack of motivation?

Living Successfully Is a Life Choice

Very few people feel good about themselves, and many peo-ple are dissatisfied with the way their lives are going. It is important to have dreams. Though being driven can be healthy and exciting, there is no reason why you can't also enjoy the pres-ent and all that it offers. I believe we should all have something toward which we are working—a dream, a goal—no matter how old we are or how successful. The key to real happiness is being able to work toward your goals and yet enjoy where you are now in your life, completely and with passion, and with constant gratitude that you are lucky just to be experiencing life at all.

The most important thing to understand about successful living is that it is available to all of us. It is almost always a choice we make. We know deep down inside what we need to feel happy, content, fulfilled, and excited about the future. Whether we are seven or seventy-seven, we probably all know what we want more of in our lives and what we would like to get rid of. With some careful introspection, we can think of what simple things make us feel good, make us feel alive and healthy, and keep us excited about life. We also know deep inside what is draining us and making us feel depressed, frustrated, and stressed out. So ask yourself, "What do I need to change or do to get more of what works on my behalf, what gets me to my goal of successful living? And what can I do to get rid of the things that drain me?" This is a good start to the self-evaluation process and to a whole new way of living!

2

SUCCESS SABOTAGE

SYNDROMES

The only things you regret . . .
are the things you didn't do.

— MICHAEL CURTIZ

There is a seventeen-year-old girl in my community who is an extraordinarily talented ballet dancer. She dances the leading roles in all the local performances. When you see her on stage, you can't help noticing her. She stands out as a beautiful young dancer with a great deal of promise. I had the opportunity to talk with her recently. Assuming she had her heart set on a professional career in ballet, I asked her where she would be studying dance when she got out of high school.

"Oh," she said, her smile fading. "I won't be dancing. I think I'm going to be an interior decorator."

"But what about your ballet?" I asked, completely amazed by her response.

She proceeded to give me an array of reasons why she would never make it as a ballerina, reasons that, I couldn't help feeling, someone had programmed into her malleable young mind. I tried to tell her how wonderfully talented she was in the few minutes we had together. Sadly, I could tell she had already given up, let go of the dream. She was demonstrating a pattern of thinking that, from here on in, would probably determine her life experience.

I've often said that if I only give my children one important lesson in life it would be this: Go after your dreams. Whatever you want to do or be, you can do it. It isn't about intelligence or even talent, for that matter, although those things certainly help. You will achieve your dream only if you know what you want, believe you can get it, and don't give up until you make it happen. We all know very intelligent people who have never achieved their dreams. How many talented people do you know who never use their talents to their fullest, if at all?

I want my children to have a healthy sense of self-esteem and to feel capable at an early age. I want them to believe in themselves. I want them to dream and to believe that anything is possible and that their options are many. As they enter adulthood, I want them to figure out what it is they are passionate about and then to focus on making that passion their future reality in spite of the competition and in spite of their possible insecurities or lack of perfect abilities. None of that matters anyway. I want them to know that they can have whatever they want if they just keep going and believe in themselves, never giving up, never letting the outside world manipulate them into second-guessing themselves. I want them to know that anything is possible for them.

Furthermore, I want them to understand the importance of balance, happiness, and integrity and that life is all about choices. I want them to pay attention to their dreams because dreams are a very important part of our identity and a great tool in defining who we are and what we want for ourselves.

Defying Success, Denying Our Dreams

Why do so many people never realize their dreams? Did they not receive these types of messages growing up? Do they not believe in themselves? Do they even know when they are sabotaging their own dreams?

Some people deny their dreams, simply because the responsibility that comes with having what they want scares them. They secretly feel inadequate. They are afraid that if they were put to the test and really had to perform, they could not live up to anyone's expectations, especially their own. Others see themselves as failures. Maybe they come from a family of failures and underachievers. Therefore, they see themselves as fitting into some family history or pattern of failure.

Many people defy success unknowingly. They sabotage opportunities that could create success even when they do appear within their grasp. They do this for myriad reasons, which aren't always clear to them or anyone else. Still others end up making choices to not go after certain dreams because they fear deep down that it could potentially be harmful to some other area of their life. These reactions often happen on a totally subconscious level.

I recognized this behavior in my own life a few years ago when I ran across some notes I had written about a dream I had. It was a dream about my being able to fly, which I am sure many of you can relate to on some level. What this dream unveiled about my career choices in the past few years was very powerful and insightful. I made choices on a subconscious level based on what I thought was best for my family at the time, without really defining it.

I feel it is so relevant to this topic that I've decided to share it with you here.

Last night I dreamed I had a flying machine. It strapped to my back and came around to the front of my body with silver tubes that pointed upward. The hand controls were on a center unit right at my fingertips. There were lots of buttons to push and I controlled everything. The speed, the height, the direction I would go, and the length of the flight were all at my command.

I would stand, run really fast, push the buttons, and up I would go. Over the trees up into the sky, to the unknown, a place that was unreachable for most people. I would stay at about thirty feet because I knew it was fairly safe there. I would still be okay if I fell. And I did fall a few times, straight down, but I would simply stand up again, take a deep breath, start running fast, press the buttons, and up I would go again.

It was such an incredible feeling moving up toward the sky. People would run after me, looking up and yelling different things. There seemed to be two different types of people. One type wanted my machine. They wanted to do what I was doing, feel what I was feeling. The other type ran after me grabbing at my feet. They were trying to pull me down. They were screaming at me that I was foolish and doing a dangerous thing.

But I just kept going, up and up. It felt so wonderful. I was

*high enough to feel the thrill but low enough to feel safe if I
fell. I remember saying to those who thought I was foolish, "If
only you could try this, and feel what I'm feeling, then you'd
know why I do it. It is such an incredible feeling."*

In reading this account of a dream I had three years ago, I am
amazed at what this says about my own career choices. You see,
I have spent a great deal of my life heading toward the sky,
reaching for the stars. But I've come to realize that there is a
price to pay for all that glory. There is a price to pay for that type
of success—a success so ominous that only few can achieve it, a
height so intense that you have to run really fast and push buttons constantly to get there. Ironically, I don't think I realized
this when I first began my journey toward following my dreams.
I thought I could do it all, have it all, and balance it all.

Then as life would have it, I became a mother. Over the
years, I have had to continuously make choices that work not
just for me, but also for my family and my marriage. I can't fly
hundreds of feet off the ground and be there for a child struggling with Tourette's syndrome. I can't constantly be up in the
air and be a wife for my husband. I can't be caught up in pushing the right buttons and still be there emotionally to talk to my
confused teenage daughter. As a result, I have made decisions,
often subconsciously, to stay grounded, even when the sky
looked so inviting and even when it beckoned me to come flying. Did I want to stay grounded? Often not. Did I not resent
taking my head out of the clouds? Sometimes. Does it mean I
won't ever end up landing on Mars and wallowing in all that
fame and glory? No. Just maybe not right now.

If you're someone who is driven, you understand that feeling of going after a dream. You understand the passion that comes with making something BIG happen. You get that feeling, almost an *addiction*, to be somebody and to do something really big with your life. It can be a blessing and a curse at the same time. Sometimes you'd like just to relax and not care, not want so much. At the other side of the spectrum are people who are not driven and do not even understand that feeling. They don't really have any dreams or goals. They just do the daily grind and live their lives. The goal I believe is to find a happy medium. We can have healthy, clear dreams and work on achieving them, while living in the moment and appreciating the now to the fullest. In this scenario, success isn't something you strive for, it is something you acknowledge daily in your life experience.

Because success is often associated with achieving our dreams, let's take a look at various reasons why our dreams don't become our reality. Some of the reasons are conscious, but many of them are not. For example, I believe I have stayed at a "safe height" in my career so that if I did fall it wouldn't hurt me or my family. As I moved closer to my lifelong dream, I began to realize that the type of success I dreamed about could make me less available in more ways than one. In retrospect, I've made subconscious choices not to go after certain things, even though they were right there beckoning to me, because their price was too high for my family to pay at the time.

This example of flying demonstrates how our dreams are affected by other variables and how complicated getting what we want can be.

Success Sabotage Syndromes

So why do our dreams elude us? Why does getting what we want seem so complicated? It's not always about fear, insecurity, and low self-esteem.

Let's look at some of the ways in which we sabotage our dreams.

Lack of Clarity

So many people go through their lives uncertain about what they want. They don't know what kind of life they want to live or even what type of career would really be best for them. As a result of not having a clear sense of direction, they make bad choices and end up working hard at jobs that don't make them happy. They end up living their lives in a way that leaves them feeling unfulfilled and empty.

Think about your parents. Did they live their dreams? Or did they do what they had to do to pay the bills and take care of the family? My father dreamed of being a musician, but he didn't have the confidence or the clarity to follow through. My mother was an artist and a wonderful writer, but she ended up working in a factory as a secretary for thirty years of her life. What happened to their dreams? I don't think they ever really thought their lives through. They just let their lives go off without any direction, careening like a car going full speed without a driver. As a result, my father was creatively and professionally frustrated, which eventually lead to his alcoholism. My mother loved life and her children, and was happy in that way, but she longed for more personal fulfillment, and she was frustrated with my father's unhappiness and drinking problems.

I see such a lack of clarity and associated frustration in my clients. I can't help feeling that much of it was inherited from their parents. If you have no role model, it is hard to understand the importance of clarifying your goals and forming a plan of action to reach your goals, skills that can and must be learned to achieve your dreams.

Lack of Motivation

You can have all sorts of wonderful dreams, but if you aren't driven or motivated, these dreams will simply stay dreams. Where does motivation come from? It can come from many desires and needs: a desire to have more, a desire to be someone, a desire to do something big, a longing for a better life, an envy of something someone else has, a strong need for control, a strong desire for change, a desire for self-improvement, a need for more security. Even fear can be a powerful source of motivation—fear of being alone, fear of being a bag lady! None of these motivators is really any better or more effective than another, and none of them is really bad or good. They just are. What is bad is if you just sit around and think about what you'd like to happen and do nothing to make it happen. Then, as they say, you don't want it bad enough. So how can you want it more? What do you need to do to motivate yourself?

For example, I never used to work out or go to the gym. I just walked when I felt like it and watched my diet. I thought that was enough. But I met a woman in a business meeting one day who changed my life. She was beautifully fit in a very feminine sort of way. She took off her jacket to reveal beautiful arms and shoulders—not masculine, just fit and toned. She had great posture and wonderful energy. She just kind of glowed every time I saw her. I envied her. I wanted to look that fit and feel that good. *She must be much younger than I am.* I thought. *That explains it.* (excuse) *That's why I don't and* can't *look and feel like that. I'm too old!* When we got to know each other better, I found out she was actually older than I! *Wow,* I thought. *I want to look that healthy and feel that wonderful. How can I do that?* I began to work out. It took about six weeks to get into the habit of it. I started to drink lots of water (another one of her secrets). Within three months, I looked better and felt better than I had in years. I could have looked at her and thought, *Boy, she looks good. Wish I could look like that. She must spend a lot of time on herself. I can't do that.* Instead I used my envy as motivation. Now exercise has become a very important part of my life and has truly changed the quality of my life. If someone else can do it, you can do it, too! How bad do you want it?

The Fraud Syndrome

It is so easy to get caught up in the fraud syndrome. It is based in insecurity and fear of failure. What if people find out that I'm really not who they think I am? What if I'm a fraud? Am I a hypocrite?

I have experienced the fraud syndrome at various times in

my own life, because I am always stepping into some new role: therapist, talk show host, and writer, just to name a few. What experience do I have? Do I have a Ph.D. in psychology? Was I an English major? Have I hosted talk shows before? No, no, and NO. But I've come to realize that many successful people didn't major in their chosen careers in college. In fact, many of them never even finished college. I've become an expert at many of these things by living the experience. If I don't know, I fake it until I do. And then I get busy getting information and becoming an expert. It is my natural instinct to be the best at what I do. I tend to overprepare, to avoid letting anyone down. I get as much information as I can, move forward, step up to the plate, and do my best. What I don't know, I'll learn.

So many people worry about being found out, that maybe they aren't as strong, smart, or confident as everyone thinks they are. I remember a therapist who came to us at the Midwest Center for Stress and Anxiety with anxiety and fear. She felt that if anyone knew she had a problem, they wouldn't want to work with her. In fact, just the opposite was true. I suggested that she share her issues with clients whom she knew had the same concerns. It was very effective. They felt as though she understood their pain. It made her more real and more approachable to them. She went through our program, overcame her anxieties, and shared her new skills with her clients.

Do the best you can, whenever you can, and don't worry about being a fraud or feeling like a hypocrite. We all have felt that way at times. It goes back to that need to be perfect and accepted completely, which is an impossible, unachievable goal anyway. Let the person who has no "problems or insecurities" be the one to cast the first stone.

Fear of Responsibility

Some of us are truly lazy at heart. Maybe we're not totally satisfied, but we don't really want to work that hard. We don't want all that responsibility. Be honest here. Would your dream really require all that responsibility, or are you blowing it out of proportion in an attempt to sabotage it before it begins? Do you not want hard work and long hours? Then maybe you need to change your dream and be honest about your desire to have more free time and less work. And that's okay. Remember, this is a time to be honest with yourself about what you want. If your dream comes with a lot of responsibility and you don't want that, it is important to be honest and accepting so that you can let go and move on to something less demanding.

On the other hand, if responsibility just simply scares you, don't let that stop you. Just keep moving toward your goal. You can handle it. Nothing wonderful comes without hard work and responsibility. When you are doing what you love you should feel motivated and energized to work hard. In fact, people who love what they do will tell you that it is almost hard to stop working and it is equally hard to let go of the responsibility when they are really into what they are doing. The good news is, when you are working hard at a desired goal, people seem to come into your life to help you with some of the responsibility. It's just the way the universe works . . . you'll see.

Fear of Failure

How many of us have tried things in the past that didn't work? How many times have you poured your heart into something, and it didn't happen? What if you spend several years working toward a dream, and it all falls apart?

I personally have experienced all these and more. We have all experienced failure on different levels. My theory is that the more you experience failure, the better you get at accepting it as an inevitable part of the life process. If you said, "Gee, I really haven't experienced that many failures in my life," I would say to you, "Gee you must not push yourself very often." I have experienced so many letdowns and failures on my path to success. I think the hardest failures are the ones when you've done something really well, and you know it's good, and you did everything you needed to do and more to make it happen . . . and it still doesn't work. That was hard for me to accept, because for a long time I believed that if you did all the right things and you didn't give up, you would eventually get what you want. Of course, for many different reasons, that's not always the case. I do believe there is a reason you were meant to go through the experience. Probably you learned something really powerful that will help take you to the next level if you just stay open and observant.

This is why it is so important to enjoy the *experience* of going after your dream. How you will go after the dream should be as important a decision as what the dream is. That way if the dream doesn't become a reality, at least you were enjoying yourself, and you learned a lot along the way. Who knows where that will take you? Often it will take you in a related direction, and sometimes in a more fulfilling way than you dreamed.

Failure is as natural as making mistakes. And the more willing you are to put yourself out there, to take chances, and to try new things, the more likely you are to experience failure. This will make you more resilient, less sensitive, and more appreciative of success when it does come along.

Fear of Success

Fear of success is a hard concept for some people to understand. How could anyone fear being successful? Sometimes the feeling is more about being undeserving of success. Secretly, people feel that either they don't deserve it, or it won't last. This often goes with bad belief systems that they have carried with them for a lifetime. They fear that they couldn't handle it if what they wanted did become their reality. Possibly they subconsciously fear it might change their life or change their relationships. Perhaps they are afraid of the responsibility success could bring.

The best way to overcome your fear of success in any area of your life is by becoming successful in another area of your life. When you experience that feeling of empowerment and affirmation, it is so wonderful that it will empower you to do more, to risk more.

I remember a man who was overweight and insecure and had fairly low self-esteem. He went through our program "Attacking Anxiety and Depression" a few years ago. As a result of dealing with his insecurities and anxieties, he overcame his problems with compulsive eating. He lost fifty pounds. The weight loss gave him a new sense of confidence, and he decided to try to change jobs. He went on several interviews and actually found a new job in sales, something of which he would never have considered himself capable of in the past. Several months after he began his new job, he called us all excited because he had decided to go to college. This was assertive for a man of thirty-four, with no previous college experience. He wrote us the most beautiful letter stating that taking that first step—losing the weight—gave him the confidence to try other things. He said the feeling of accomplishment was so great after losing the weight that it was a shot of confidence. With each challenge and conquest, he felt a bit apprehensive, a bit amazed, and then he felt energized. I remember him saying, "I would try this, and say, 'Gee, maybe if I can do that, I can do *this*, too,' and I would try it. I just give myself permission to try it now."

Allow yourself to be a winner. Give yourself permission to have success, money, nice things, good friends, and a healthy body and mind. You deserve it, and good things do last if you nurture them. Success feels good, and it's addictive.

Life Changes

One thing you can be sure of is that your life is going to change, often when you least expect it and sometimes in ways you don't like. But with change can come new opportunities. Many people have become successful entrepreneurs because they were forced out of their jobs or because they decided to go into business for themselves for one reason or another. Many women have become successful business owners because they became mothers who wanted to get out of the system and have more time for their kids. You never know where life changes will lead you. Just don't let them stop you. Look for the opportunity. It's there. Maybe this is what was supposed to happen to lead you closer to your dream.

Take my anxiety disorder as an example. Who would have

thought, way back when I was suffering so horrifically, that I would end up creating a program for treating anxiety and depression that would be used all over the world? Who would have thought it would have led me to build my own company, to write books, and to appear on television? Look around. Is this change something you can use to help you go after your dreams?

The "I'll Be Happy When . . ." Syndrome

This syndrome is probably the second most common reason we sabotage our dreams, even when we've achieved them. We get caught up in thinking that until we achieve our dreams completely, we can't be happy. I think this makes it almost impossible ever to achieve your dream because, even if and when you do, you still won't be satisfied. You've gotten so used to the bad habit of being dissatisfied that when you finally do have what you want, you won't know it or it won't be enough.

I know a brilliant, talented woman named Teresa, who is extremely successful in many ways. She owns a thriving business, she is in a good marriage with a supportive husband, she has three healthy children and a beautiful home, and she is financially secure. And yet, she doesn't consider herself successful. When we talked, I asked her why not. She said until she had reached a certain financial level, she wouldn't think she had "made it." Anyone else would look at her and say she *had* made it. She had everything and plenty of it, but in her mind she was deficient.

This can be confusing, because I am suggesting it is healthy to have goals and to strive for them. The key to real success is to set goals and strive for them but to still be happy in the moment, enjoying your present life. Don't delay happiness until your goal is achieved.

If Teresa could enjoy her daily life and feel fulfilled and could use her feelings of financial frustration as motivation to push herself to diversify and expand her company, fine. Maybe this drive to have more financially would force her business to a new level, and that is not a bad thing. That could be the catapult that gets her where she wants to be. But I see her frustrated and stressed out all the time. She is already pulled in too many directions and doesn't seem to be balancing any of it well. She is worn out, distraught, and feeling like a failure—no good energy for growing or even running an existing business. And what if she never achieves her goal? Will she waste the next several years pushing herself and agonizing over not being where she wants to be? Will she consider herself forever a failure? Wouldn't she be ahead if she were to relax a bit, work on what she is passionate about, and still allow herself to enjoy the life she has right now? Her company is secure and profitable. She can continue to expand and to look for new ways to add to the bottom line. In order for her to be content with the present moment, she needs to let go of the constant pressure.

She isn't thinking about her daily life experience at all. She is so caught up in having more that she is working and pushing too hard. She isn't enjoying her present moment. She isn't having fun anymore. She said she will be happy when she reaches her financial goals. She is making the mistake that so many of us do. She is becoming a victim of the "I'll be happy when . . ." syndrome. With some careful thought, she might realize that what she really wants, she already has, if she would just allow herself to appreciate it. She wanted financial security (she has it, but she thinks she needs more), time for herself (which she could take if she would spend less time jumping through hoops trying to get to "happy"), and more peace in her life (which she could give herself if she would let go of the pressure). I think she believes that once she achieves her financial goals she can finally relax and live the life she wants. The irony is that she could be living the life she wants right now if she only clarified it and gave it to herself.

If you can say, "I eventually want to achieve this, but in the meantime I can be happy and enjoy my life the way it is now because *now* is all there is," the journey to get what you want will be a pleasant one. The energy around you will be good, and it will draw good things and positive people into your life. When things are hard, you'll keep going because you are basically happy, and even challenges and setbacks can't affect that. It gives you stamina and patience. If you are caught up in believing that you can't be happy or satisfied till you get to a certain place in your life, you will be more likely to walk away or to give up out of present-moment frustration and unhappiness.

Envy and Jealousy

It is easy to let envy and jealousy make you second-guess yourself. These two negative emotions can wreak havoc on our dreams. If someone else gets there before we do or in a grander style, it can make us feel incapable and discouraged. We worked harder, did more of the right things, deserved it more. Why bother? I say: "Don't go there. It is so destructive." Instead, use envy and jealousy to motivate you to keep going. Do you like what someone has or is doing? How can you emulate something that they did to get there? What can you learn from them? How can you use their success as motivation to move you closer toward your goal? That is all that envy is good for after all.

I remember going to visit my sister Donna and her husband in California when I was a teenager. As children we grew up poor in an old brown house with old furniture. She and her new husband both worked for a few years in Ohio, saved some money, and then moved to northern California. They bought a beautiful, small, new home and nice furniture. I'll never forget walking into that house when I was fourteen years old and looking all around. I was overwhelmed and in awe. We never had things like this growing up. I didn't think people like us could have things like this. I specifically remember the eggshell, buttery soft leather sofa they had in the living room. *Wow*, I thought to myself. *If she can do this, maybe I can, too. Yes, we come from a poor family, but that doesn't mean we can't have nice things someday. That doesn't mean we can't have class, style, and a beautiful home.* I really believe Donna set the trend for the rest of us kids. She showed us that it could be done, so we all followed suit. We have all found success at different times in our lives and in different ways. It hasn't been without various levels of sibling rivalry, but Donna showed us the way. We could have turned this into negative jealousy and envy that would have destroyed our sibling relationships, but instead it motivated us.

I remember when our "Attacking Anxiety" infomercial had been out for a few years. A woman by the name of Susan Powter came out with a new diet infomercial, and it was hugely successful in a very short period of time. I remember people in the business asking me why I thought her show was so big, and why ours wasn't doing the same kind of numbers. I speculated but I didn't know for sure. Ours was working well and was very steady. I did sit back and watch her success with a bit of awe and admiration and, okay, a bit of envy. I had heard she had made a lucrative book deal based on her infomercial appeal. *Well, if she could do that*, I thought to myself, *so can I*. My infomercial had been on for several years and has been quite successful. On the heels of her book's success, and probably to some degree as a result of hers, I went out and created my own book and landed a wonderful book deal. Since then, my book, *From Panic to Power*, has become one of the best-selling books ever written on anxiety, and my infomercial is still on the air, after ten years. Powter's show has come and gone, a few times; and knowing her, she'll be back again. Instead of turning that envy into negative energy, I used it as motivation to make my book dream a reality.

Can you see how easy it can be to sabotage your own happiness and success with insecurity, bad belief systems, jealousy, and negative thinking? Can you see how easy it would be to spend a lifetime waiting for the right time and circumstances to live your life your way? It is so easy to make excuses for why we don't get what we want.

When you think back on your life and your dreams and desires, consider what you wanted to do or be that never came to be part of your reality. And then ask yourself why these things didn't happen. Do an honest evaluation. I suggest you write it in your journal. Were you not motivated enough? Did you not feel capable? Did you fear failure? Did you fear the responsibility and life changes that success could bring? Did you secretly fear that you weren't good enough or talented enough to make it?

How to Sabotage Your Sabotage Syndromes!

It is time to turn your excuses into a powerful plan of action to help you achieve your dreams. Here are some steps you can take to overcome the sabotage syndromes you have created for yourself.

1. Do an honest evaluation of the sabotage syndromes that you are using now or have used in the past. If they aren't listed in the discussion, create your own. Write them in your journal. Begin to recognize your own negative dialogue with yourself, and write it in your journal.

2. Make a strong commitment to beginning to eliminate these syndromes from your list of bad habit behaviors. Simply do not allow yourself to use them anymore. Ask people who know you well—a spouse, your "power-partner," a good friend—to let you know when you are sabotaging your own potential or making excuses. (See item 4 regarding a "power partner.")

3. Replace your sabotage syndromes with positive empowering thoughts and actions that will lead you closer to your goal. Start using this energy to begin setting goals and focusing on what you want. We will be discussing this in more detail in chapter 8, but you can begin using some of the following empowering replacement thoughts immediately, to overcome self-sabotage now.

- I am smart and capable, and I am comfortable with success.
- I want a certain lifestyle, and I am capable of achieving it.

- Even though I may want to strive for more, I am happy and grateful for now.
- It is okay if I fail or make a mistake. It is part of the life process.
- It is okay to feel insecure at times, but I won't let it stop me from trying.
- I know I can define my goals and form a plan of action. I just need to start, be patient, and stay positive.
- I don't need to always be perfect and do everything right.
- I can handle responsibility.
- I deserve to be successful and satisfied.
- Change doesn't scare me. It offers opportunity for growth and new adventure.
- I don't need to be jealous of anyone else. There is enough abundance in the world for everyone. I will use my feelings of envy as motivation.
- It is okay and healthy to ask for help and support.
- I have a right to my dreams and desires.

4. Pick a "power partner." This person should be a friend or mentor with whom you can share both your dream ideas and your sabotage syndromes. He or she should be a positive person whom you respect and admire, a cheerleader of sorts who wants you to achieve your dreams. Use this relationship to help you stay motivated and on track.

5. Begin to form an empowerment mantra (a "power paragraph") of who you are and why you can have what you want. This should be a short paragraph made of sentences that make you feel better, comforted, and stronger. I suggest you

write a paragraph that addresses all the sabotage syndromes you use. An example might be as follows:

I deserve success. I am creative and intelligent and very capable of handling anything that comes my way. I embrace change as an opportunity for something new. I know what I want, and I am motivated to get it. I will create opportunities, and I will follow through and make them happen. I wish everyone around me success and happiness because that only brings more positive energy into my life. I am lucky and grateful to have my life now, and it is okay and healthy to desire more.

This is just an example. Please feel free to use this one, but I strongly suggest you write one for yourself that addresses your specific syndromes.

Be Sure That You're Going in the Right Direction

As we move through life and strive toward certain things we think we want, often our desires change. Possibly we realize that what we thought we wanted wasn't what we really wanted after all. In fact, in talking with people who have achieved great things, I found many who said that once they achieved their lifelong goal, they felt disappointed and almost depressed. What looks good in fantasy isn't always what it is cracked up to be. And sometimes the more we have, the more we want—whether it's money, success, or material things. We lose our perspective even when we truly have enough to live the life we want. That is why it is so important to enjoy the experience of going after your dream because maybe that will be the best part of the process. And, you may spend a great deal of time there. If you are going in the right direction, time spent in pursuit of your dreams will feel right and enjoyable. In fact, that is one way to tell if you are going in the wrong direction and not following your heart. If you are not enjoying the trip, if you are burned out, exhausted, and unhappy in your struggle to achieve your dream, something is wrong. Maybe you are going about it the wrong way. Possibly you are trying too hard and not allowing the universe to work with you. Or you could be subconsciously sabotaging your own success. Or maybe you're going after a dream you think you want, but in reality, you don't. Whatever the reason, burnout and frustration are clear signs that closer evaluation is necessary.

What Makes You Feel Good?

What makes you feel motivated, excited, and happy? What makes you feel peaceful, content, and fulfilled? Whatever is working for you, you should strive for a life that offers you more of it. If your dream became a reality, would it take you in that direction? Does whatever you're dreaming of having or doing promise to give you more of what works for you? These are serious questions to begin asking yourself in your quest for true success.

3

PERSONAL SATISFACTION

My crown is in my heart, not on my head.
Nor decked with diamonds and Indian stones.
Nor to be seen: My crown is called content;
A crown it is that seldom kings enjoy.

— WILLIAM SHAKESPEARE

Have you ever watched a young child walk through a big toy store in an attempt to pick a special toy? The child walks down every aisle, carefully browsing through the shelves, touches everything, picks things up, and even rides things through the store if possible.

Recently, I was in a Toys R Us to purchase favors for my son's birthday party, and I saw this scenario: A father and his young son were walking around the store. It was clear that the father had offered to buy his son a special toy as a reward for good behavior. "What do you want?" the father asked. "I don't know," the small boy replied. The child wandered from section to section, his eyes getting bigger and bigger. "Come on, Steven, pick something out. We need to go." The father was obviously growing impatient. "I want this, this, and this," said the little boy, "and this, too." The father looked irritated. "But what do you *really* want?" said the dad. "I don't know," said the child again. I did my shopping and watched with sympathy as the frustrated father followed the child around the store from aisle to aisle. With his son unable to make a decision, the angry, frustrated father decided to leave, dragging a toyless, crying little boy behind him.

Do you realize how much time and frustration the father could have saved himself if he had sat the child down *before* they got to the store to discuss what in particular the child *really* wanted? Then they would have been on a mission to get something specific. They could have gone to that particular department, bought the toy, and avoided the added confusion. Instead, they wandered in, clueless, and then were surrounded by so much stimulus that the child couldn't possibly make a decision. As he wandered, he got more and more confused.

When we are young adults, life to us is like a toy store to a child. It is big, exciting, and a bit overwhelming, with lots of choices. Sometimes it tugs at us just to play and have fun. And there are so many choices that it's easy for us to get sidetracked. It is hard to stay focused or to be sure of exactly what it is we want. If we aren't clear about what we want in every area of our lives, we could end up like the little boy, frustrated and sad, wondering why we're constantly coming up empty handed.

Do You Know What You REALLY Want?

It is so important to know who you are and to know what brings you joy so that you can *choose* to make it a part of your life every day.

So, what do you really want? What would it take for you to

feel personally satisfied? Do you even know what personal satisfaction is?

Successful daily living—choosing to live in a way that is satisfying—is an art form. It is all about the choices we make. I am amazed at how few people have learned how to paint, color, and design their lives to their specific liking. In fact, people are so busy being busy that they've forgotten about quality of life on a daily level.

Personal satisfaction is hard to define. We all know people who are professionally and/or financially satisfied and yet feel something is missing in their lives. They don't even know what it is. Many people describe a feeling of emptiness, aloneness, or unhappiness for no particular reason that they can define.

So what is it that makes a person feel satisfied? The answer isn't specific, it isn't black-and-white. Different people have different needs. Some people need an amount of physical attention that would make others feel smothered. Some people thrive on chaos and constant activity, whereas others prefer calm, predictable, relaxed surroundings. Some people can't feel personally satisfied unless they are accomplishing something. Others feel satisfied only when they are enjoying their personal time doing something they love to do.

To me, personal satisfaction is contentment—nothing is missing, things are good, life is a pleasure, and I am grateful and fulfilled with the experience. You must *choose* to live a life that makes you feel content.

Recently, my family and I moved to a small town near the ocean. Whenever I go anywhere, to the grocery store, to the bank, to my children's school, I see the waves crashing on the sand, I smell the salty air, and I see the sea gulls gliding on the wind. It is truly a spiritual experience for me. It is a simple thing, but it turns the most mundane drive into a precious moment. It is something I wanted most of my life, and we finally made it happen. This is just one example of something I've chosen that provides me with a great sense of daily personal satisfaction.

What does personal satisfaction mean to you? There is no right or wrong answer here. What is important is that you determine what it would take for you to improve your levels of personal satisfaction in various areas of your life.

Do you like where and how you live? Do you like your home and your surrounding community? Do you like how you spend your personal time and the people with whom you spend it? As you read this, are you already making excuses in your mind as to why you couldn't *really* live the life you want?

Let's take a closer look at the things we've been talking about here, which fall under the category of personal satisfaction. *Personal satisfaction* is an intriguing and difficult subject to address. It is such an intimate thing. Can it be described or, better yet, defined?

In my attempt to do so, I have divided personal satisfaction into eight specific categories. I'm sure there are more, but these categories are general enough that everyone can relate to them. To set the mood for each specific category, I have chosen to use beautiful passages or quotes taken from works of some of my favorite writers or other interesting people from the past. These brief selections from people dating back to the 1800s demonstrate beautifully that throughout time people have been searching for and pondering the meaning of contentment.

I can think of nothing sadder than to live a happy life without recognizing it.

—PETER SCOTT,
The Eye of the Wind

I believe that personal satisfaction is associated with maturity, integrity, self-acceptance, realistic expectations, and spirituality. Unfortunately, I don't know many people who are truly satisfied. They often seem to feel that something is "missing."

I know people who have become ministers because they felt something was missing, and I know people who have quit the ministry because they felt they were missing something. I know people who have walked away from their children because they felt the need to fill a void; they were compelled to seek fulfillment elsewhere. I know people who have *had* children because they felt a void needed to be filled. The problem is that when people feel empty, they often look outside themselves to fill that void. Often the void lies within our experience of life. Do we expect too much? Do we settle for too little? If we take some time to analyze our expectations, we might find we can do quite a lot to improve things for ourselves.

Categories of Personal Satisfaction

I believe it would be helpful to analyze the eight categories of personal satisfaction that I mentioned earlier. I don't know that it is possible to achieve long-term, total, personal satisfaction, but I do know that it is possible to feel *more* satisfied.

Let's start with your life right now. If you aren't satisfied with some areas of your life, now is the time to take a close look at all the categories of personal satisfaction and to make some positive changes. Take a look at your satisfaction levels regarding these categories and see what you need to work on.

Home

How often, on a December afternoon, when outside the red glow of sunset sinks behind the iron woods, and the ground mists rise, have I entered the old cottage, and, before the blinds are drawn, or the room is lit, have I paused to watch the play of rosy light on walls and ceiling. It flickers under the old rafters, and draws new colour from rugs and cushions. Now of all times can one indulge in reverie before that ruddy glow, a pleasure scarcer and scarcer in these hurried days. The comfortable old arm chair, the feet on the fender, a cat, if you will, coiled up on a cushion, and a brass kettle singing on the bar, with a glint of light falling on bellows, toasting-fork, and chestnut roaster, spoils of visits to the antique shops, these are the symbols of home, and induce that pleasant melancholy of the reminiscent mind.

—CECIL ROBERTS, 1935,
Gone Rambling

Your house, apartment, or condominium, your dwelling place should offer you a feeling of welcome, warmth, and intimacy. It should look and feel good to you. It should provide you with a sense of calm, comfort, and safety. You should like spending time here, and you should enjoy bringing others here. Your home should be your refuge, your place of peace and happiness, your shelter from the outside world.

I have filled our home with warm, cozy things. There are lots of flowers, little fountains, pretty pictures, and soft furniture. The surroundings are warm and comfortable. Often in the morning, I'll make a fire in the family room fireplace and light a few candles, even on school days. *(Do you realize how many people never use their fireplace? Are you one of them?)* On Saturday mornings, the kids come down to find music playing all around the house, sometimes classical, sometimes rock and roll. Sometimes it's even Christmas music in July. Why? Because we all love Christmas music, that's why. It makes us think of snow, and fires, and holidays, and family gatherings. Sometimes on Sunday mornings, we make pancakes and dance around. I know my kids love to get up and come downstairs to this warm, cozy environment. It makes us all feel good.

You don't need a lot of money or fancy things to make a warm home. You don't even need a fireplace. As I mentioned before, I grew up in a brown-shingled house at the end of a deadend street. Even though the house was old and the furnishings were meager, I do have some pleasant memories. I remember on Sunday mornings, my dad would get up early, set the radio to the big band sounds of Glenn Miller and Benny Goodman, and begin making Swiss steak for Sunday dinner. He started cooking early so that the meat would be good and tender. The smell wafted through the house and twisted up the stairs to our bedrooms. The music woke us all up, and we stumbled down the stairs whining and complaining. And yet, I cherish that memory. Even now, when I think back, I can feel the warmth associated with that smell.

On those same Sunday mornings, dad would sometimes take me with him to the little corner store to buy sticky, pecan rolls. Occasionally he would buy my brother and me a kite. We had a big open field next to our house, and I can still remember running and flying kites with Mike on a crisp, cool, spring morning.

Our old house had floor vents that blew strong gusts of hot, soothing air in the winter. I can remember coming in from the snow to the curtains blowing, warm with heat, as I took my place on the heater vent and had intimate conversations with my mother. These are my memories.

You are the adult now. You can surround yourself with whatever your heart desires. What type of environment do you want for yourself? What memories would you like to have for yourself and your family? If your level of dissatisfaction is high regarding your home, you need to change it. Make some notes here. What simple things could you do today to change the atmosphere and make your home more appealing for you?

Could you add a garden, paint the walls, or add a stereo? Could you begin to make special family breakfasts on Sundays or do family readings from a special book on a certain night of the week? How about one night when the whole family cooks dinner together? These are just a few suggestions. What would you and your family enjoy?

Community

I am in love with this green earth; the face of town and country; the unspeakable rural solitudes, and the sweet security of the streets.

—CHARLES LAMB

For many years, we lived in Ohio in a very small farm town—population 3,000. Many of the locals drove around in pickup trucks and wore baseball caps. People were simple and friendly. They held the Apple Festival every October and chicken barbecues on Sunday at the local firehouse. It wasn't cosmopolitan. There was no movie theater or shopping mall, but the town had its own beauty and appeal that I appreciated. It was quiet and peaceful. The "Ohio" grass and various garden flowers smelled wonderful on a summer day. And I loved the weeping willow trees that surrounded the community. Many of the homes on Main Street were beautiful old brick houses with character. A river ran behind the old farmhouse we lived in, and we had fresh apples from the apple tree in our backyard. We knew we wouldn't stay there forever, but we made the choice to enjoy the time there to the fullest.

The place where you live, your town, should offer you a sense of belonging. It should bring you simple pleasure just to live there. It should offer you the lifestyle you desire. It should be a place you enjoy seeing every day. Your town or city should offer you a sense of social community. It should be a place you enjoy walking in and driving through, with smells, sights, and sounds that make you feel good. It doesn't have to be big and fancy or small and rural. It has to be what you want it to be. And maybe it already is, but you just aren't seeing it or taking advantage of it. Beauty and interesting people are everywhere.

Recently, my husband, David, and I were fortunate enough to be invited to a private screening of a documentary that was directed and written by our friend Todd Robinson. It was the story of a ballerina from New York named Marta Becket who opened an Opera House called "Amargosa" in Death Valley in the middle of the Mohave Desert! Here was a place of complete and total desolation. It is dry and barren, with very little community to speak of, and yet she saw the beauty there. This extraordinary woman, who, I am guessing, is in her seventies, chose to make this little town in the middle of nowhere her home. There happened to be an old, run-down theater. She purchased it, took several years to paint it with dazzling artistry, and made it a showplace for her own private recitals. Now, people come from all over the world to see Marta perform her one-woman show. Her husband, who at one time was her handyman on the property, sometimes performs with her. Here is a woman who had a dream and followed it. She had lived all over the world and performed in some of the most prestigious theaters in the country, and yet, she chose to live in a small, isolated town and to build her own little dream. She seems completely and utterly satisfied with her choice of community and her life.

If you are dissatisfied with your community, what could you do to change that? Is moving an option? Is there somewhere you have always wanted to live, but you haven't given yourself permission or even think it is possible to live there? How could that become a realistic and attainable goal for you? If you really cannot move at this time, you must find ways to appreciate your community. Get more involved in local activities, join a church or a social or political group, reach out and talk to people at social or sporting events, take walks to appreciate the surroundings more. Get to know the people. Lower your expectations of what your community should be and enjoy what it is. Every place has something to offer.

Personal Time

"To execute great things a man must live as though he had never to die." Agassiz lived in this way. . . . He never had an hour in his life when he was not pleasantly occupied; and he innocently wondered, when the people he met in society sometimes complained of being bored with life. Every contrivance to kill time appeared to him the funniest of all jokes. "Time!" he was wont to exclaim; "my only trouble is that I have not enough time . . . I cannot understand why anybody should be idle; much less can I understand why anybody should be oppressed by having time hang on his hands. There is never a moment, except when I am asleep, that I am not joyfully occupied. Please give to me the hours which you say are a bore to you, and I will receive them as the most precious of presents. For my part, I wish the day would never come to an end."

—EDWIN PERCY WHIPPLE, 1887,
Recollections of Agassiz

How do *you* spend your daily personal time? Do you treasure your time? Do you treasure yourself enough to give yourself the gift of time? You should make time for yourself in the morning. Give yourself time to relax and enjoy your morning. Get yourself off to a good positive start. Find a special time and place to enjoy your green tea. You must make time throughout the day to sit and relax and feel peaceful. Your day should include time for yourself during the morning, afternoon, and evening, whether it's time spent reading, working out, or driving a good distance in your car. You need time to be yourself. And what you do with that time is just as important as having it. For example, when you are driving in your car, you should enjoy the ride, listen to your favorite music, talk radio program, or some great tapes. You should be "joyfully occupied." Don't shortchange yourself by being irritated and in a hurried frame of mind. This is your time. Make it pleasurable.

All my life, I've owned a convertible. I just love cruising with the top down, enjoying the smell of the air and the feel of the wind. For me it's the difference between sitting in a hotel room looking out at the beach or sitting on the beach with your toes in the warm sand, feeling the sun caress your body. It's the difference between sitting in a ski lodge watching people ski or being on a pair of skis flying down the hill, smelling the snow, and feeling the wind on your face. Choosing to drive a convertible is a daily quality-of-life choice I've made. Every day, it turns part of my personal time, which could be a short drive to the store or a long drive to a meeting, into something wonderful. A drive in that car can be a peaceful mind-clearing experience or an exhilarating joy ride, whichever I am in the mood for.

If you aren't enjoying your time or if you are bored, ask yourself what is missing in your life. Do you need a hobby or could you volunteer? Don't sit around and be idle. Don't waste time watching television by the hour. Read, paint, or write. Go spend time with someone who needs company. Use your time as the precious gift it is.

Health and Physical Appearance

Health doesn't insure happiness; but there's not much happiness without it.

ANONYMOUS

You could have all the money in the world. You could have beautiful homes on each coast and diamond rings for every finger. You could have designer clothing and fabulous cars. But if you were sick with some horrible terminal disease, none of it would matter at all. You'd give it all up in a second to have your health back. I know; I have worked with people in this exact situation. All you would want is your health. The irony here is that we literally kill ourselves everyday, stressing ourselves out to have money and the things money can buy, and so few of us do anything to keep ourselves healthy.

Do you exercise regularly? Do you take care of yourself nutritionally? Do watch your diet and maintain a healthful weight? Do you get regular checkups? You go to work every day, take care of your house, balance your checkbook, and get your hair cut. How can you ignore the most important thing you have, your health? How can you give it such little attention when, without it, you'd have nothing?

How Bad Do You Want to Feel Good?: If you are healthy, you should look and feel healthy. You should feel energetic and ready to get up in the morning. If you are in fairly good health, you should be able to walk a good distance without tiring. You shouldn't feel tired all the time, and you shouldn't need a lot of caffeine to give you energy. If you feel tired often, possibly you aren't getting enough exercise. Exercise is a must for feeling and staying healthy, and it must become part of your daily routine. It is impossible to feel really good without regular exercise. If you are making excuses for why you aren't exercising, stop it. Get up and get going. Figure out what you like to do and just get started. You don't need to buy expensive equipment or join an expensive gym. You can simply walk, run, or exercise in your living room. How bad do you want to feel good? You will be amazed at how regular exercise helps eliminate feelings of depression, anxiety, and stress, and at how empowered it makes you feel.

You should be conscious of the "stuff" you are putting into your body. Do you drink caffeine and alcohol to the extreme? What's extreme, you might ask. I believe that two cups of coffee a day is unhealthful and that drinking alcohol every day or night might be cause for concern. No one who is relaxed and healthy and feeling good physically should need excessive amounts of caffeine and alcohol. Let's face it, we drink caffeine because we need energy, and we drink alcohol to relax, to take the edge off. If you understood nutritional deficiency and how it affects your body and if you understood the importance of exercise in overall good health and feelings of well-being, you would do more to take care of yourself, and you wouldn't need the caffeine and the alcohol.

The Midwest Center recently began selling a new audio program that is all about nutrition and was created by Dr. Ron Meyer and Dr. Joel Swabb. It is called "Break Free." My motivation to become involved in this product was my own struggle with emotional mood swings because of premenstrual syndrome (PMS), as well as Sammy's Tourette's syndrome, and the tendency of Brittany, my teenage daughter, to get tired easily.

I always knew that nutrition plays a major role in good health, but I was amazed at how little most of us really know about nutrition. It is so much more than just taking vitamins and eating protein. A nutritional deficiency can manifest itself in many ways that could actually cause you to want to drink alcohol, eat junk food, and slam down caffeine on a daily basis. It is believed that poor nutrition is at the base of many disorders, including attention deficit hyperactivity disorder (ADHD) and depression. Of course, it is believed that poor nutrition plays a major role in the development of such diseases as heart disease and cancer. Once you understand the importance of good nutrition and you gradually make changes in your life, you'll be amazed at how much better you feel. Become informed. Read books, order the "Break Free" program, but do something to educate yourself and to take control.

Your physical appearance is important because it makes a statement about who you are and how you feel about yourself. If you are confident, you probably dress well, have good posture, and convey comfortable body language. You probably maintain a healthful weight and enjoy looking good in your clothes. You should like what you see in the mirror even if it isn't perfect . . . it never is. If you don't feel good about the way you look, it is hard to be confident or even to enjoy life fully. It is fine to want to change something about yourself. Take a long hard look at yourself and ask yourself what you would like to change; then look into changing it. It's your body, and you need to be comfortable with it and feel good about it.

I remember a woman I knew when she was in her seventies. She was beautiful and full of energy, but she wasn't thirty anymore. She said she felt pretty good about herself until she looked in the mirror. She didn't like the wrinkles, and that chin thing was happening. She thought about surgery but decided it was not something she wanted to do. I suggested she start exercising to firm up her body and to raise her spirits, not to mention what it would do for her health. She took my advice. She also decided to color her hair and try a new style. We went shopping, and she bought some stylish, trendy outfits that she typically would not have worn. Within a few weeks she felt better and looked better. She smiled more and stood more erect. She just needed a few changes.

Sometimes the simplest things can make a world of difference. Don't waste any more time feeling bad about the way you look or cheating yourself of feeling physically fit. Make plans to take control of your body and your health beginning immediately.

Relationships

And before long my closest friend was Joseph Wood Krutch, hereinafter to be known as Joe. Many times since then I have tried to date the moment when I knew this to be true. I think it was one evening when the two of us stood in the vestibule of a subway train bound for Times Square, to a restaurant, a theater, or both. The train was noisy so that we had to shout, but the circumstance seemed unimportant. The important thing was that we had a great deal to say to one another, and that each was really interested in what the other said; also, that each was eager to speak when it came his turn, and was confident that what he said would be worth hearing. We like those who inspire us to talk well, to talk indeed our best, which in their presence becomes something better than it ever was before, so that it surprises and delights us too. We like least those persons in whose presence we are dull. For we can be either, and company brings it out; that is what company is for. Joe Krutch from this moment was famous company for me, and the conversation begun then has never stopped. It has ranged without apology from the grandest to the meanest subjects; it has a natural facility in rising or in sinking; but the point is, we have never run out of things to say.

—MARK VAN DOREN, 1958,
The Autobiography of Mark Van Doren

Relationships are a very important element of a truly successful life. Friendships with people you know well, enjoy, and trust are crucial to a happy life. We all need a person with whom we can be ourselves completely and who still loves and enjoys us. We should have nothing to hide, nothing to pretend to be, when we are with this person. A good friend who understands and appreciates you, and you them, is an invaluable resource for pleasure. We sometimes need different friends for different things. You might have one friend with whom you talk intimately, and another friend with whom you discuss your kids. Possibly you have another friend at work and other friends you enjoy with your spouse as part of a couple. It is particularly good and important to have a friend who motivates and inspires you to be the best you can be.

If you don't have any good friends you should ask yourself, why not? Possibly you don't trust people, you are afraid of intimacy, or you think it's too much work to establish and build friendships. No effort is more fruitful. Good friendships have been known to save marriages and heal terminal disease. Possibly, you are so busy working and taking care of your family that you don't have time to build friendships. Take time. Pick a few people you would like to know better and start spending time with them. Ask them to dinner, a movie, or whatever. It does take time to build a friendship, but you must take the time. You must make the effort. It is difficult to feel fulfilled and happy no matter how professionally successful you are if you don't have friends to share it with.

The passage at the beginning of this category ends with the words: *we have never run out of things to say.* This is how it is with my husband and me. We sit for hours talking about everything from the children, to business, to reminiscing about memories from our past. We enjoy each other's company. It is the same with my daughter, Brittany. I love to just sit and talk with her about anything and everything. It makes me smile to watch the excitement in her face as she describes her day and talks about her life.

I believe we all need family. If you are single, it would be wonderful to form a surrogate family—a group of people with whom you feel strongly connected, people to whom you can turn and on whom you can depend, and who can depend on you. If you do have a partner, do what you can to nurture the relationship; it is one of the most important relationships in your life. No one has a perfect partner, or marriage, or husband, or wife. Do what you can to help the union stay strong, and look for the positive side of what you have. Honor and cherish your children, parents, and siblings. No, they aren't perfect, but they are blood. It doesn't get any more intimate than that. If there are problems, get help for yourself, and get help for them if you can. Life is too short to get all knotted up in the stupid stuff. But remember, you can't "fix" everyone. You can, however, continue to love them.

Expectations

Yesterday afternoon I went to the Cliff with Henry Thoreau. Warm, pleasant, misty weather, which the great mountain amphitheatre seemed to drink in with gladness. A crow's voice filled all the miles of air with sound. A bird's voice, even a piping frog, enlivens a solitude and makes world enough for us. At night I went out into the dark and saw a glimmering star and heard a frog, and Nature seemed to say, Well, do not these suffice? Here is a new scene, a new experience. Ponder it, Emerson, and not like the foolish world, hanker after thunders and multitudes and vast landscapes, the sea or Niagara.

—RALPH WALDO EMERSON, 1838,
The Heart of Emerson's Journals

I have often said my appreciation for the simple things in life comes from my mother. It takes very little to make her happy and joyful. She appreciates her family, the world around her, and life in general. In fact, I love taking her places with us because she gets so excited about everything. She will sit in the back seat of the car, telling stories about her childhood and growing up on a farm, while my kids hang on every word. As we drive along, she points out the most mundane things and makes them exciting to my eight-year-old. "Look at that beautiful old farm house. Look over there, Sammy, those trees look like pencils, so tall and narrow, with a point at the top. What kind of tree do you think they are? Look at the sunset, isn't it pretty? Just looks like God himself painted a beautiful picture up there." Sometimes when I get caught up in the rat race of life, I call her and just say, "Hey mom, what are you doing right now?" In a matter of seconds, she takes me to a simpler life, a quieter place, where less is more.

What do you expect out of life? Are you constantly setting yourself up for disappointment? Can you be happy and content just sitting and watching the sunset or losing yourself in a favorite song? Take a minute and look around right now. What is in your line of vision that you could enjoy in some simple way? As I write this, I myself am looking out at our wooden porch swing. I have spent many wonderful moments there with my children reading and talking. This to me is personal satisfaction.

Spirituality

For all his learning or sophistication, man still instinctively reaches toward that force beyond . . . only arrogance can deny its existence, and the denial falters in the face of evidence on every hand, in every tuft of grass, in every bird, in every open bud, there it is.

—HAL BORLAND, *The Best of Success*

Going through life would be very empty and dissatisfying without any spiritual connection and support. So many times in my own life my spiritual beliefs were what motivated me to keep going when everything appeared to be falling apart. It is important to feel connected to and even responsible to a higher power—someone or something to turn to, have faith in, fall back on, when nothing else seems to be the way it should be. Spirituality gives you a clear sense of right and wrong and an understanding of the power of love in the world and of that fact that everything good stems from this love. If you have a sense of spirituality, you will see yourself as part of this loving energy and recognize that all that you do should come from this place. This understanding will save you so much unnecessary grief and turmoil.

If you are lacking a sense of spirituality, I suggest you try going to a place of worship and reading some books about the type of spiritual experience to which you want to feel connected. One of the best things you can do to find your spiritual place is to talk with your friends. Many of them are doing different things in their own search for spirituality. You might want to check out what they are doing and see how it feels to you.

I am Christian, and I attend a Protestant church. I have a new friend who is very much into Buddhism. When I was visiting her one evening, I noticed she had created a beautiful home altar. She told me that she and her family meditate regularly, even her five-year-old son. I was intrigued. She invited my family to attend her "church" on Sunday with her family.

The shrine was a beautiful place where all sorts of people came to worship, pray, and meditate. In fact, for the first twenty minutes of the service, everyone sat in silence and meditated. Then a monk, who was quite funny and full of modern-day insight, gave the service. After the service, we walked around the lush grounds. I watched in amazement at the rituals her young children embraced with ease and comfort. They prayed and mediated as if it were second nature. It made me think how meditation might be helpful to my children in providing them with a sense of peace, unity, and godliness.

You choose whether to have faith and be spiritually connected. Not everyone feels he or she needs this source of support and guidance, but I would be weak and lost without it. How about you? If you need to fill this void in your life, do it now. Keep an open mind and an open heart, and see what appeals to you.

Integrity and Self-Worth

To be nobody-but-yourself in a world which is doing its
*   best,*
night and day, to make you everybody else,
means to fight the hardest battle which any human being can
*   fight;*
and never stop fighting.

—E.E. CUMMINGS

Nothing gives you more confidence than knowing you operate from a place of integrity. Integrity is simple. It makes you like yourself. You feel good about who you are and why you do things. You feel good about yourself when you go to bed at night. You make decisions based on your integrity. It isn't always easy to do that, but it is gratifying to know that in the end you still like who you are, you can be proud of what you do, and your family and the people in your life who trust and love you can be proud of you as well. You don't compromise in a world full of compromises. You don't sell out. You are valuable and worthy and strong in your convictions. Integrity is self-worth.

Maintaining my integrity has been one of my most valued assets, as well as one of my life's biggest challenges. So many times in the business world especially, temptation creeps in like a nasty, dark wizard, offering everything you ever wanted for a price. The question is this: How much are you willing to pay? And if you don't give in, will it come again? If you maintain your integrity, will you find success? In my own journey, if I can't do it and maintain my integrity, I don't do it. Opportunities come and go, but once you lose your integrity, you lose your center, your sense of self-worth.

If you don't feel good about yourself, there are things you can do to change that. Decide right now to start being honest, especially with yourself. Don't compromise your belief in what is right and wrong. Start making decisions based on these beliefs. Do something to make the world a better place. Volunteer and give your time to someone who needs it. Get involved. You'll begin to feel your energy changing, and so will others. This will give you an inner sense of power because you believe in yourself and in principles that almost act like a shield to protect you. It is as if no one can hurt you because no matter what they do they can't take your integrity away from you.

Choose to Be Joyfully Occupied

As you can see, so much of successful living is about choosing how to live in every moment and choosing a way of life that makes you feel good. You might be thinking things like, *Everyone can't afford a convertible.* To that I would say, "Why not? If I did it, anyone can do it. No one gave it to me. I made it my reality." Maybe you're thinking, *Not everyone wants to live by the ocean, or learn how to meditate.* I'm certain this is true. These are examples from my life and other people's lives, things from someone else's wish list. You have your own . . . I hope. If you are already justifying why you can't do what you want, or live the way you want, it might be a sign that you *are* sabotaging your dreams. You've probably gotten very good at justifying why you can't have things or change your life. This is a form of self-sabotage. Recognize it for what it is, right now, and get rid of it so that you can begin to form a plan of action to make your dreams a reality.

Personal satisfaction is different for everyone. If you are young, you might want life to be exciting and stimulating, offering opportunities for power, success, romance, and passion. On the other end of the spectrum, if you are retired, you still want the romance and passion, but you probably aren't as concerned about "making it." Your idea of success might be a relaxed, secure, less pressured life, doing what you want to do. You may long for more relationships in your life or better health. No matter, you still have choices to make about what successful living, happiness, and contentment mean for you now and in the future. You need to look at all the categories of personal satisfaction closely and apply them to your life. Maybe you need to work on establishing close relationships in your life. Possibly you need to enhance your spirituality. Maybe your health and fitness need improvement. If you feel a void in any of these categories, you're getting a perspective on what you need to work on for your own sense of personal satisfaction. How badly do you want to feel better about your personal life? Are you willing to do the work to get you the results you desire?

Think back to a time you wanted something so badly, you knew you'd do anything to get it, and you did. I am sure you used a certain type of energy and thinking process to get what you wanted. You might have been uncertain and a bit insecure about your ability to get it, but I bet you were focused and determined. You probably used visualization, prayer, and positive self-talk to bring it to you, although you might not have realized it at the time. These are all skills we are going to be fine-tuning in the following chapters of this book. This is the kind of cumulative positive energy needed to acquire or to achieve great things, whether it is a goal of losing weight, building a multi-million dollar company, reaching out to make new friends, or changing a low self-image. The power begins with thoughts, which create action, which creates change.

The following Bill of Rights for personal satisfaction should help you to clarify your desires:

- You have the right to be excited about your life.
- You have to the right to create an attractive, comfortable home.
- You have the right to live wherever you choose.

- You have the right to have healthy, rewarding friendships.
- You have the right to have romance and passion in your life.
- You have the right to feel attractive and healthy.
- You have the right to be proud of who you are and stay honest with yourself.
- You have the right to spend time with and on yourself.
- You have the right to find your own spiritual path.

Time for Clarity

So what do you want your daily life to be like now? In five years? In twenty years from now? As you look back over these categories of satisfaction, realize that anything can be changed and improved if you so desire. It's not too late, you're not too old or too young, you're not unworthy or stuck. It is your life. These are your life choices. You must know what you need to improve before you can establish a plan of action to do so. So keep evaluating. You are on the path to long-term successful living.

4

PROFESSIONAL

SATISFACTION

The higher prize of life, the crowning fortune of a man,
is to be born with a bias to some pursuit which finds him
in employment and happiness.

— RALPH WALDO EMERSON

What Do You Want to Dream?

Do you remember a time when someone asked you what you wanted to do or be, and you were enthusiastic and excited about the answer? If you are like most people, you could list the skills you've accumulated during the past ten years, but when it comes to knowing what's in your heart, what you'd really love to do, you haven't a clue. Most of us have lost the ability to dream and the motivation to pursue those dreams.

The truth is that we were born to dream, but somewhere along the way, our dreams died. Maybe you tried to follow a dream once, and you never quite achieved it, so you gave up. Perhaps you've tried and failed, possibly more than once, so you decided not to put yourself through that pain again. Maybe you think you're too old or it's too late. Maybe someone gave you messages that you weren't good enough. Or maybe you've fallen into a comfort zone in which you're paying the bills and getting by, and you don't want to rock the boat. You can stay stuck there forever and probably get along, but if you've forgotten how to dream, if you're not doing something you enjoy and pursuing a goal, you may find it difficult to be motivated and excited about your life now or in the future.

So how about you? Are you excited about what you do and are you looking forward to your professional future? Is it obvious to others that you enjoy your work?

One of my favorite comedians is Robin Williams. If you've seen him, and you'd have to be a hermit not to have, you can't help watching him "work." He is truly talented. Professional satisfaction comes so naturally to him, and he is enjoying it so much, that you forget he is actually working. He pulls you into his world and summons you to watch him perform his craft. I always watch in amazement. He is obviously doing what he loves and loving what he does. It is magical to see. When I watch him, I find myself envious of his talent and the fun he is having.

I take my dog Maggie to a pet grooming service when I am too lazy or busy to bathe her myself. Allen, the middle-aged man who grooms her, is such a pleasure to experience that I look forward to taking Maggie there. Allen has a way with Maggie and with every other dog he cares for. He talks to Maggie in a special way to which she responds. He has a special nickname for her, and he always turns her over and rubs her tummy. He sings and dances when he is bathing the dogs and talks to them as if they are children. He makes everyone smile. I swear

Maggie breaks into a grin when she sees him! It is a treat to watch the way Allen relates to animals. He, too, pulls you in to observe his craft.

My husband, David, runs the direct marketing division of our company. He wheels and deals and networks at all the medical conferences. He reads constantly about anything and everything that is related to what we do, and he thrives on taking the company to new levels. He loves it. He talks about what he does with great pride. He is excited about the future and our potential. Anyone who meets him is impressed by how much he knows and how much enthusiasm he has for our company. I think it is fair to say people are in awe of his ability to enjoy his work so much.

Professional Success versus Professional Satisfaction

Professional success means different things to different people, and I believe it is different for men than it is for women. Most men associate success with money, power, and material things. I asked twenty different men from different socioeconomic backgrounds to describe the most successful man they know, and they all described someone who has done well financially. They talked about the money he has made or makes, the way he lives, and especially about the things he owns as defining factors in determining his success. Certainly, Robin Williams fits those criteria. But what about Allen, the dog groomer? Is he not professionally fulfilled? Anyone who knows him would say he absolutely is. Could it be then that professional fulfillment is as much about getting satisfaction out of what you do as it is about money and status?

When I asked women to describe a successful woman they know, most of them described someone who had a satisfying career and a healthy personal life. It was interesting that many of the women with whom I talked felt that women are happiest when they have both a full personal life and a career they enjoy. Women seem to equate success with all-around personal and professional fulfillment, healthy self-esteem, and a sense of security.

Although many people think they are clear about what it means to be professionally successful, recent studies indicate that as much as half of the employed population is professionally frustrated. Does this mean that professional success and professional satisfaction are two different things? Absolutely. A recent article on America Online (AOL) News referred to "Career Depression Syndrome" and stated that it is becoming an epidemic in the United States. According to Dr. Jotham Friedland and Dr. Sander Marcus, two psychologists who have named this disorder, of people who seek career counseling, more than half suffer with the disorder. Symptoms include career unhappiness, self-doubt, discouragement, feelings of inadequacy, hopelessness, and depression. The article goes on to say that women experience this as often as men, and that it is seen in every type of profession from factory workers, to lawyers, to psychologists and teachers. Even people with careers that most people would think of as successful are suffering with the syndrome.

The article stated that there are three stages to Career Depression Syndrome:

Stage 1: Career dissatisfaction

Stage 2: Career demotivation

Stage 3: Career paralysis

When you are in stage 1 and 2, you feel unhappy and stuck, and it is hard for you to stay productive and motivated. By the time you reach stage 3, your personal life is being affected and you are depressed. You may even dread going to work and become ill. You may wonder what is wrong with you and begin feeling down, guilty, and unmotivated to do anything, from going to work to socializing.

I believe professionally frustrated people do things at this time that they normally wouldn't do because they do not understand that what they are really dealing with is career dissatisfaction. They often drink, overeat, and even have affairs in an attempt to feel better. If they would recognize their career dissatisfaction for what it is, they could take steps to do something about it and make some changes. Once they stabilize and improve their professional life, other areas of their life would become more satisfying as well.

Professional satisfaction can be defined as employment that you are in because you want to be and because you enjoy the work you are doing. Does it matter if what you do involves status, high salary, and great benefits? Only if these things matter to you. There are no right or wrong answers. We are not here to judge someone else's desires and needs. You are here to figure out what you want and need to feel satisfied in every area of your life.

Let's take a look at the categories in the area of professional satisfaction that are relevant to this book and important to consider when you are evaluating your own life. As you go through these categories, remember that this is an opportunity for you to evaluate your individual situation. If you don't work or if you are currently unemployed, this chapter can be particularly helpful in clarifying what you do want for yourself professionally, should you enter the workplace in the near future.

Get out your journal and a pen or pencil, and remember to read the following categories from a personal perspective.

Sense of Fulfillment

If you work for a living, your job should be something you enjoy and look forward to doing. It doesn't matter if you are a tile installer, a computer programmer, or a freelance writer. You should get up in the morning anticipating your work with a sense of pleasure. In other words, it is important to look forward to your day and what you are going to be doing with it.

If you are like most people, you spend *at least* one third of your twenty-four-hour day working. You spend more than half of your waking hours doing whatever it is you do to make a living. Let's hope you are enjoying it! If you aren't, there is definitely a problem. Why are you there? Why are you doing what you are doing if it doesn't bring you pleasure and fulfillment on some level?

Sing, Dance, and Be Merry

This past summer my husband, David, and I took our first cruise. One of the ports of call was Ocho Rios, Jamaica. We booked a ten-mile ocean-kayaking excursion that took us to some magnificent places. We stopped at waterfalls and jumped into cold springs. It was a wonderful experience. What I remember most, when I think back on that trip, were the four Jamaican men who were our guides on the excursion.

They were in the lead kayaks and carried fresh fruit and juice for us to enjoy when we stopped. What was interesting about these men is how happy they all were. They laughed full-bodied laughs, and they sang and danced in their kayaks and out. They made the trip very special. It was clear they weren't dancing and singing because they were "supposed to," they just wanted to. They told us they perform at night locally when they can, and they work as kayak tour guides during the day. They took so much pleasure in singing, harmonizing, and dancing among themselves. It didn't matter to them that we were there or whether we were watching them. They were just making the most of their moment.

I remember that our tour took us past the mayor's home, which was waterfront and quite opulent. They all talked about his beautiful home, but they didn't do it with envy. I don't think they envied anybody. They were enjoying their experience and happy to be in it. I'll never forget how contagious their positive energy was for the rest of us. Once again, we were pulled into someone's craft.

Are these Jamaican men professionally fulfilled? You bet. To be professionally satisfied doesn't mean that you aren't working toward growth or advancement. It doesn't mean that you don't want to be more or have more someday. It simply means that you are enjoying what you are doing right now. Possibly you are on a path to a bigger, more challenging career; possibly you are in a part-time or even temporary situation. You can still be fulfilled and excited in your experience. I wouldn't take a part-time or temporary situation that didn't offer me these things on some level, so why should you? And if you are in a permanent situation that doesn't offer you these things, then it is time to reevaluate.

Sense of Achievement

We all need to feel that we are talented and capable. We need to feel that we are accomplishing something and doing something of value. Most people have jobs because there is a need that has to be filled on some level. You do something that provides a service of some sort, whether you are a dentist or a repair person working for a phone company. It is important that you feel good about what you do. It is so rewarding to feel a sense of achievement at the end of the day—that what you set out to accomplish that day got done, that you are valuable and that your work has value. If your job is one that offers no sense of value, that in itself could be the source of your dissatisfaction.

If you aren't working at all, possibly you are feeling as if *you* have no sense of value, which can lead to depression. This can be especially true if you are older or alone.

I know two women who are both in their seventies. Martha is retired and stays home, living alone. She reads the paper, watches television, talks on the phone, and does little odd jobs around her home. She gets bored. She often complains of feeling useless and lonely. Barbara, on the other hand, works part time at the local school where her grandson is a student. She's a lunchroom and playground monitor, and she works in the school library. She is always up and happy. As a result of working at the school part time, she feels needed, spends time with her grandson, makes some extra spending money, and makes a difference in a lot of children's lives on a daily basis. These two women have made different choices. One is unhappy and depressed; the other one is fulfilled and looks forward to her days.

A sense of achievement means different things to different people. For some, it means doing something well. For others, it might mean accomplishing certain goals. For still others, it means doing something that makes a difference. You need to know what achievement means for you and pursue a career that gives you the opportunity to fulfill it.

Make the World a Better Place

I love what I do because I feel it makes a difference. It puts positive energy out into the world. I am reminded of the wonderful children's book *The Lupine Lady*. It is about a young girl whose grandfather tells her that whatever she does in life she should do something to make the world a more beautiful place. She lives her life and travels the world. At the end of the book, she spends her days as an old woman sowing lupine seeds all around. It's a simple thing, it's a simple book, but a powerful message. I believe we are all here for a purpose. I also believe that the purpose is often right in front of us, but either we are too blind to see it or we choose not to. I think we struggle and suffer so that we can find a solution and share it with someone else. I have often been told that the reason someone recovers from anxiety using the skills I teach is that they know I've been there. I have lived the experience and come out to the other side.

I know a remarkable woman named Kathy, who is a very busy personal assistant to a big producer. Several years ago, she was diagnosed with breast cancer. She actually had it twice. Since her recovery, she has helped thousands of women around the world deal with the fear and the anticipation of breast cancer treatment. By lecturing, writing, raising funds, and more, she has made a difference in the world. I am convinced it has helped her in her own recovery. She is on a mission. She has maintained her career as a production assistant, but she has formed a second career on the side of reaching out to others. She is professionally and personally satisfied.

Look for ways you can make a contribution to the world, keeping in mind that the most valuable gifts you can give are probably your time and your compassion.

Opportunity to Use Your God-Given Talents

You, my friend, are very talented. What are you good at? Are you a good writer? Are you good with people? Are you good with your hands? Could you sell snow to an Eskimo? Do you love working on the computer? Maybe you love kids or you enjoy being outdoors. Possibly you thrive on challenge, and wheeling and dealing is a special talent you have. Maybe you are good with numbers or you are a great organizer. Do you even know what your talents are? Think for a minute. You know yourself. You know the particular skills that you have. Let me make it clear that I am not saying you are a pro or well trained in something, just that you know what your interests and talents are. If you are a pro or well trained in something in particular, that's wonderful! How can you use those skills to make your dreams a reality?

I know my talents. I am a good artist; I can paint and draw things. I am good at decorating and design. I am a great speaker and motivator, and I can really entertain people. I am a very good salesperson. I can sing, and I write music. I am great with kids, and I've even been referred to as a pied piper of sorts. Kids follow me around, and we do silly things.

I am a good writer. (I hope that is obvious). If you had asked me in high school to list my talents, I would never have listed writing. I hated typing class. I didn't see the point in it. I knew I didn't want to be a secretary. It never occurred to me that I might write books some day. I didn't particularly enjoy English. I knew I enjoyed writing poetry and memoirs, but that was about it. I didn't really know I could write until I tried it. I remember writing the first three chapters of my first book and sending it off to my editor, Diane Reverand, at HarperCollins. I was scared to death that it wasn't good enough, grammatically correct, or whatever. She was very pleased. She liked my direct, down-to-earth style. It was confirmed—I could write.

It is important that your career offers you the opportunity to use your talents and the opportunity to improve and to stretch yourself. You need to feel that you are good at what you do and that you have the opportunity to grow.

Have Fun

I know a very powerful, successful agent who rides around in a car all day taking meetings and talking on his cell phone. I asked him once what he does for fun, and he thought for a moment and said, "You'll think I'm weird." I assured him that I already thought he was weird, and I continued to prod him for an answer. "Okay," he said, "I'll tell you. This—this is fun to me." He smiled and motioned around the car, extending his cell phone. "I love being on the phone doing deals and taking care of business." It is such a pleasure just to sit and watch him work, to hear him on the phone, and to watch his body language. He is so professionally satisfied it is enviable.

Sense of Self-Worth: Would People Want to Watch You Work?

Have you ever watched a jewelry maker create a necklace right before your eyes? Have you ever watched an artist put a brush to some paint and create something incredibly beautiful with seemingly very little effort? Have you ever watched a hair stylist give a really good cut? Have you ever seen a good electrician install an extensive stereo system? Have you ever seen a computer programmer handle a computer with the same type of familiarity that a great musician would use to handle his instrument? These are truly wonderful things to observe.

Once again, you are pulled into what these people are doing. You are compelled to watch them. In fact, that is a great way to tell if people are professionally satisfied. Watch them. They will move confidently. These people become intensely involved in their work. They lose themselves in what they are doing. It becomes a dance, and observing it is an honor. These people are great examples of professional satisfaction.

Work should be fun. You should get so caught up in what you do that time goes by unnoticed. You should get pleasure in talking about your career, and people should enjoy watching you do it, even if it is a simple thing. Your pleasure and level of involvement is what makes it interesting after all, whether you baby-sit or run a large corporation. Would someone enjoy watching you do your job? If you think the answer is no, then maybe it is time for a change.

I remember one of the best baby-sitters my kids ever had and the pleasure that it was just to watch her with the kids. Ann was like a great orchestra conductor. She picked up her baton the minute she opened the door and let you in. There was the string section—the small babies. They were in a brightly colored crib filled with wonderful mysterious things. There were the percussions—the three-to-five-year-olds. They were loud and bold, playing games in her wonderful sandbox just outside under a tree. There were the wind instruments—the flute and the horns—the little four- and five-year-old girls who played dress up and danced around. Ann was organized and skilled in her ability to manage and direct these kids. They all loved her. At Christmas, her home was magical. The kids were in awe. They loved going to Ann's, and Ann loved taking care of them. Every new baby, every new little brother or sister, was anticipated by all the kids, all the parents, and anyone else lucky enough to be part of the community Ann created.

She knew what she was doing, and why she was doing it.

She provided a service, and it was much needed and much appreciated. She was so good, in fact, that she had a waiting list. People waited for months to get into Ann's place. She had a healthy sense of self-worth and valued her skill and her profession. This was what she wanted to do with her life, and it was obvious.

Know What You Want and Know Where You're Going

If you don't know where you are going, how can you possibly get there? You don't even know what your final destination is. Moreover, if you don't know where you are headed, how do you know you are in the right place now? If you don't know what your long-term goal is professionally, it will be difficult to handle the work, the stress, and the pressure that comes with any profession.

If you are on the path to your future long-term goal, what you go through to get there is justifiable. You have to pay your dues. If you don't know where you're going, or worse, if you are going in the wrong direction, you will be continually frustrated and irritated. You'll be looking for all the reasons to justify why you are unhappy.

Making Money, but Misdirected

When I first began to give seminars, I joined a national organization for speakers and trainers. Through the organization, I met a new friend named Mathew. We both started our speaking careers at about the same. He was excited to go to all the meetings, and he got busy working for bureaus all over the country. He was traveling three or four days a week. He was sure he wanted to be a speaker trainer. It was his long-term professional goal. Although we shared the dream to some degree, I remember feeling confused and uncertain. I certainly wasn't as enthusiastic as he was. He began sales training sessions for major companies. I began doing stress management seminars for big corporations. I was quite good, and my reputation spread by word of mouth. I was traveling and giving full-day seminars. He was doing the same. Although I was making great money, I was getting resentful of the time I spent traveling, and I felt the full-day seminars were too time-consuming. I didn't have time to do anything else, like write, produce, and work with people one on one, all the things I loved doing.

He loved everything about the profession, and he was thriving in every area of his life as a result. I was thriving financially, but I was personally and professionally unhappy. I did some soul-searching to determine what I wanted. I finally figured out that I didn't want to be a full-time speaker and corporate trainer, even though I was good at it. It wasn't going to get me to my long-term goal of being a writer, producing my own television show, and working with people one on one. I limited my speaking engagements to keynote presentations only, and I began to spend the bulk of my time writing and producing and working with people individually. As a result, I've become successful doing things I truly enjoy.

In retrospect, I remember talking with Mathew and hearing his enthusiasm and wondering what was wrong with me. Nothing was wrong with me. It just wasn't my dream. Thank goodness I figured it out, or I could have ended up in a very frustrating profession. Though I would have done well financially, I would have been constantly complaining and wondering why I was unhappy.

It makes me wonder how many people end up in careers simply because the money was good or the opportunity presented itself. They settle in and work hard, and, before you know it, time passes. They become frustrated and dissatisfied and look around for other opportunities, but they are afraid to break away. Or possibly they make the change and still end up frustrated and dissatisfied. Did they ever bother to ask themselves what they really wanted from a career?

Guidelines for Professional Satisfaction

Here are some guidelines to help you move beyond professional frustration to achieve professional satisfaction.

1. *Make a list detailing your talents.* This list should include any skills you have acquired through the years as well as any God-given talents you have, even the ones you aren't using or have never used professionally.

2. *Write a detailed description of the perfect job for you.* It is important to be creative but realistic. It's not likely that you'll be president of the United States, but if that is a real aspiration of yours, go for it! In your description, be specific about the hours you would work, your salary, the type of work you want to do, the level of responsibility you would want, for whom you would work, and so forth.

3. *Think of two phone calls you could make today* that would move you closer to your perfect job, and then make them. This will get you started. Call someone who is doing what you want to do and arrange a lunch to discuss your ideas. Call a bank about financing your own small business. Call someone you know who knows someone you need to know. You get my drift.

4. If you are currently employed and frustrated, *make a list of your frustrations*. Is it possible that these frustrations could be resolved, offering you job satisfaction in your current situation, or is it clear that you are simply unhappy and you need to make a change? If it isn't quite clear, share the list with your power partner, and ask his or her opinion. Trust your gut—you probably know the real answer.

5. *Become your biggest fan.* Begin to believe in yourself and your dreams again. Fill your thoughts with all the reasons why things *can work* instead of sabotaging your life and dreams with all the reasons that things will go wrong. Stop making excuses and start making plans.

I just read an article in *Los Angeles Magazine* about a 104-year-old man who recently won a medal for shot put. He said he didn't start working out until he was 100! He now has a manager and an agent, and he was even on David Letterman's show. So what do you want to do when you grow up? It's never too late.

The following Bill of Rights for professional satisfaction should help to motivate you:

- You have the right to have a career.
- You have the right to enjoy your job every day.
- You have the right to change careers at any time in your life.
- You have the right to acquire new skills.
- You have the right to be the best you can be.
- You have the right to set goals and go after them.
- You have the right to make your own decisions.
- You have the right to work part time.
- You have the right to be proud of your work.
- You have the right to design your own professional life.

The Defining Moment

You need to know what your long-term professional goals are and to work in a career that takes you there. Do you want to be in management or to own your own company? Do you want to have more free time and less responsibility? Do you want to achieve a certain professional status or make a certain level of income? Where do you want to be in five, ten, and twenty years, and is what you are doing now going to get you there? If you don't know the answers to these questions, you need take a hard look at what you want personally, professionally, and financially. Then you need to take a look at your talents and to ask yourself what changes you need to make to help you get what you want on these various levels.

The interesting thing about personal, professional, and financial satisfaction is that you must take them all into account to clarify any of them. What you determine you want for yourself on a personal level will determine to some degree what you want professionally. If your personal time is important to you, if you are a parent or are married, for example, you may not want to travel or work late hours. This kind of thing is important to know when you are making career decisions. It is extremely important that you are honest with yourself. If you don't want to work long hours, you probably shouldn't pursue a management position with a big firm. If you want to be available to your children, you probably shouldn't pursue a job that calls for extensive travel. If you don't like pressure, you probably shouldn't be in sales.

More important than knowing what you don't like is knowing what you do like. Whatever you do professionally should provide you with the opportunity to do what you enjoy every day. Given the current economic climate and the fact that unemployment is at an all-time low, you have no excuse! Get out there and get the career you want. Be who and what you want to be from this moment on. Stop compromising. Life is too short and too much fun to live it any other way!

5

FINANCIAL SATISFACTION

Nature gave man two ends—one to sit on, and one to
think with. Ever since then man's success or failure has
been dependent on the one he used the most.

— GEORGE KIRKPATRICK

The "Haves" and the "Have Nots"

Some people believe there are two different types of people in the world: the "haves" and the "have nots." The "haves" are the ones who, you've probably guessed it, *have* things. They have nice homes, new cars, great clothes. Some even have personal gardeners. They take great vacations and have lots of money in mutual funds. They are financially satisfied. The "have nots" struggle. They don't have the things they want or the lifestyle they want, and many of them don't have long-term financial security.

What is interesting is that sometimes, the so-called "have nots" get good at justifying why the "haves" are unhappy, selfish, or unworthy. Over time, the "have nots" can become bitter and negative. They often justify why they wouldn't want what the

95

"haves" *have* anyway. "They're phony or pretentious. Their value system is screwed up and they're too materialistic. They work so hard to 'have' that they're stressed out. I wouldn't want to live like that." It is a very basic way for the "have nots" to justify their own financial dissatisfaction.

Of course, nothing is that black-and-white. There are many people who live simple lives and are quite content with what they have. But I do think there is some merit to this concept of the different attitudes of the "haves" versus the "have nots." The key is to determine which type of person you are and to ask yourself if you are happy there. Are you satisfied with your life and the things you have, or would you like things to be different? Would you like to live a different lifestyle or to have more?

If you feel that desiring or having things is bad, selfish, or materialistic, you may be a victim of the "have not" complex without even knowing it. The problem with this type of thinking is that it will actually prevent you from having. Ask yourself this question and answer it honestly: Are you justifying your own lack by criticizing others who do have and enjoy things?

There is nothing wrong with wanting and enjoying material things, unless of course "things" are all you care about, which probably isn't the case for most people who have nice things. I know many successful people who have beautiful things who are also very grounded, loving, and well balanced. If you recognize your own denial and then allow yourself to desire things, you can proceed to the next step of allowing yourself to have things. This is a big step toward getting what you want materialistically and otherwise.

I am certain I spent a good part of my life as a "have not." I was somewhat jealous of things other people had while I was growing up. I felt as if I didn't fit in or belong in certain places. I felt inferior. I know my father was a "have not." He envied people who had nice homes and nice things because he couldn't afford them. Instead of using his envy as a source of motivation, he constantly belittled things other people had and found ways to insult the people who had them. That message was very confusing to me while I was growing up. I knew I wanted a different life than the one my parents had, but I didn't know how to get it. I had no role model for success or achievement. No one in my family was all that successful or had much in the way of material possessions. My sister was the first one to purchase a nice home and fill it with beautiful furnishings, which, as I mentioned earlier in the book, helped me to realize that our family was capable of having.

My father's constant negative comments about people who were successful made me feel that success was a bad thing to desire. He also spent a great deal of time criticizing things that people had, things that I thought were quite wonderful and even desirable. I ended up feeling unworthy, confused, and guilty for wanting more.

This type of upbringing greatly affected my self-esteem. For example, there was a time in my life when I didn't think I was good enough to shop in an expensive department store. I remember feeling that surely the store clerks knew I was unworthy. My father was a car salesman and my mother worked in a factory, so I was discount-department-store material. And besides, only materialistic, pompous, insensitive egomaniacs shopped there anyway. I didn't want to be like that . . . did I? See how our opinions and ideas evolve?

Then, something happened in my life that changed my perception of myself, and my potential for living a better life, forever. I went from being someone who wanted to be a "have" but thought of myself as unworthy to someone who believed she could be and was determined to become a "have": I was a freshman in college. A new friend of mine invited me to New York City to visit his parents. Once we arrived, I was in awe of everything. Richard was very worldly and sophisticated, unlike me or anyone in my family or anyone I had known in my life up to that point! I remember going to expensive restaurants with Richard's family, restaurants without prices on the menu where several people waited on your table at once. I remember vividly walking into Saks Fifth Avenue with my sophisticated friend beside me. Richard's attitude of entitlement and confidence was becoming contagious. I think it was one of the most powerful turning points in my life. It was okay to pick things up at the counter. It was fine to fantasize about the fancy clothing. I could walk through the designer department and say "Just looking," and no one would throw me out. I liked it, and I wanted more of this type of experience. But if I wanted it, I had to be the one to make it happen. I had to allow myself to want it and then to go after it. This certainly wasn't something I inherited.

That time spent with Richard in New York was the beginning of my motivation for a certain type of lifestyle, a certain level of financial satisfaction, and an attitude of achievement that, even though it took several years to manifest, has been part of my life ever since. It ended up being the catalyst that has motivated me to take great risks in my life and to open doors to new experiences I only dreamed about growing up. It has also been part of the driving force that has helped me have a successful career and build a successful company.

The topic of financial satisfaction is somewhat controversial because there is such a broad spectrum of what people want or need to feel satisfied. Let's be honest. Most people like money. They like the things money can buy—homes, cars, better health care, and so forth. Most people need to feel secure, and money offers them that sense of security. We all want to pay our bills and have money set aside for unexpected emergencies, but financial satisfaction goes way beyond that.

Financial satisfaction includes such considerations as lifestyle, material possessions, the ability to maintain daily and monthly expenses, and the ability to invest money and to save for the future. It is impossible to be financially satisfied if you are carrying substantial debt from the past, if you don't feel you have enough money to enjoy your life now, and if you don't feel financially secure about your future.

The Doers and the Drifters

In my work with individuals and corporations during the past fourteen years, I have encountered two types of people: (1) people who plan their life and are strongly motivated to get what they want, and (2) people who drift through life with no clear sense of direction. The drifters end up frustrated and have a hard time establishing a sense of true happiness, satisfaction, or security. Maybe choosing a path and becoming successful sounded too difficult initially, so they chose what they thought was the easier path. Perhaps they tried different careers, wore different hats, and left their careers up to chance, choosing what they considered to be the easiest journey, the path of least resistance. Taking this route is actually what I call "the path of most resistance."

The irony here is that when we leave our lives to chance,

when our dreams aren't clearly defined, and we have no specific plan of action, we end up frustrated. We find ourselves doing things we don't enjoy just to achieve a certain sense of "security" that we never seem able to attain. We constantly feel dissatisfied and insecure because it is impossible to be strongly committed to anything that isn't in our hearts. The very path we thought would be the easiest way is actually fraught with unnecessary battles, often lasting throughout our entire lives. Along this path, we fight incessantly with our inner selves, wondering why we are not excited, stimulated, satisfied, or content with our lives.

The first type are the planners, movers, and shakers. They are goal oriented and know exactly what they want. They are clearly on a forward path, and they want to achieve. In the past several years of meeting and working with successful people, I have observed several characteristics that the successful have in common: They are driven. They know what they like, they know what they want, and they are willing to do the work and take the risks to get it. In my observation, many people who are financially successful and satisfied had a desire to be so from an early age, even if it was subconscious.

Programmed for a Life of Prosperity or Poverty

Do we subconsciously categorize ourselves as children into a certain economic social class? Are we programmed at an early age to expect a certain type of lifestyle for ourselves as adults? I believe this is true for many of us.

A very compelling commercial has been airing on CNBC

lately. Although I am certain it is meant to be humorous, it also makes a strong statement about the long-term effect that family upbringing and surrounding environmental influences have on a person. It profiles twin baby boys who were separated at birth. One boy goes to live with a modest family from a lower social economic class. In the commercial, he is shown spending his time through the years hanging out with his unmotivated parents and watching television. The other baby boy goes to live with a family who subscribes to the *Wall Street Journal*. The commercial then follows each boy briskly through life, demonstrating that by they time they are twenty-six years old, their lives have turned out to be quite different. The first boy still lives with his parents in their modest little house. We are led to believe that he is living a dull, uneventful life as a dependant underachiever. The second boy spent his time reading the *Wall Street Journal*, setting goals, and challenging himself. He grew up to be a self-made millionaire with a beautiful home and an interesting life. Now as corny as this seems, I believe it does hold a thread of truth.

Recently, I was working with a group of teenage boys. I was fascinated to hear their different attitudes about their futures. One of the boys, whom I'll call Michael, had parents who were successful entrepreneurs. Both parents were fulfilled professionally. As a result of being self-employed, they were able to spend much of their time with their children, Michael and his younger brother. His father coached all his sons' sports activities, and his mother was very involved in their school. They took interesting family vacations, and the parents spent lots of time playing and having fun with their kids. They encouraged Michael to understand the value of money, and they encouraged his independence and responsibility. Michael considered them great parents. He was very proud of them, and it was clear that he considered them wonderful role models.

Another boy, whom I'll call Greg, had parents who had never gone to college and never had professional careers. His dad was a carpenter and had changed jobs off and on throughout his life. His mother worked a few times but never really focused on any one thing. They lived in the house Greg's father had grown up in, which Greg's father was leasing from Greg's grandfather. They lived a very simple life. Greg's father worked twelve-hour days and often came home tired and frustrated. He complained about his job and was constantly angered about his lack of control and feelings of being unappreciated. He spent most evenings having a few drinks and watching his favorite television shows. Greg's mom was always tired and sad. She didn't know why, but she found it hard to motivate Greg to do anything, from doing his homework to cleaning his room.

When we talked as a group about future goals and dreams, it was interesting to hear the difference in the boys' expectations of themselves. Michael was very excited about the idea of going to college, and he hoped to get into an Ivy League school. Not going to college clearly wasn't an option he had considered. He wanted to own his own business or to be in the banking or investment business. What amazed me is how familiar he was with the stock market and how knowledgeable he was about business in general. It was clear that this young man was motivated, had dreams, believed in himself, and was going to be financially successful.

Greg, on the other hand, was not motivated. He spent much of his group time justifying why college wasn't important. "My dad didn't go to college, and he has done okay," he said. He didn't realize that his family's security came mostly from his grandfather. His dad could not have afforded a home on his own. His dad was far from financially satisfied or what one might term "financially secure." As a result of his family's financial struggles, Greg could not afford to go on special school field trips. He could not afford the clothes or the things that others kids had. Because of this, he spent a great deal of time justifying why things that other kids had were overrated. He was already learning how to justify his financial dissatisfaction. He had probably learned how to do this from listening to his financially dissatisfied parents. He had no experience or role model for success or satisfaction. In fact, he had the opposite.

This is a sad example of the influence our surroundings have on us as we are growing up. It doesn't mean that a child like Greg won't grow up to be successful. Some children from lower income backgrounds end up extremely driven to achieve, but many don't because they fall into a pattern of thinking inherited from their parents. Many of these kids are terrible with money, and they don't understand the importance of financial security or financial satisfaction because they've never been exposed to it. They don't understand the importance of having a life plan, setting goals, and being committed. They often drift through life.

Children often learn about motivation and self-esteem by watching their parents. The good news is that we can change our motivation to be successful by exposing ourselves to achievement or to a better life. Often just experiencing the pleasures and perks of a better life makes one want to be and do more, just as it did for me when I went to New York.

There is a fine line between motivating kids to be achievement oriented and keeping them from becoming overwhelmed and misdirected. Schools are pushing kids to learn more, study harder, and to be more responsible. In working with high school kids, I have found many of them are already so overwhelmed by existing peer competition that they are insecure about their ability to deal with competition as adults in pursuit of challenging careers. There is immense anxiety associated with choosing a career path. Should people follow their heartfelt dreams? Or should they choose a more realistic career path that would offer predicted financial security and the best future job opportunities? Are we unwittingly leading our youth toward skills and desires based on perceived future financial opportunities to the exclusion of passions that might fulfill their hearts *and* their pocketbooks? Should one choose a future path simply because it appears to offer security in a seemingly insecure world? If they do, will they spend the better part of their lives compromising?

These are difficult questions to answer. To evaluate your life and what is important to you so that you can choose the right career path and goals, these questions must be considered. The balance comes in combining your dreams with realistic financial desire. You determine your individual financial satisfaction needs by determining what you want for yourself because the truth is that most of what you want takes money.

How Bad and How Fast Do You Want It?

You may love to paint, but if you want to live in a large home, drive a nice car, and travel extensively, a career as an artist might not offer you what you want financially, at least not for a while. Maybe that is okay with you. Maybe you could satisfy your dream and achieve what you want financially by realigning your plans a bit.

I know a woman named Alisa who is a gifted artist. Though she loves to paint and has talent, she wanted to live a certain way. She likes traveling and having nice things. Her painting didn't offer her enough income initially, and she knew it would be a long time before it did. She decided to become a makeup artist in Detroit and eventually worked in New York. She made upward of $1,000 a day. She did well and enjoyed her job. She was able to use her talents as an artist, and she also enjoyed the travel and social life her job offered. Eventually Alisa met and married Paul, and eventually they had three children. She quit her job and spent her time mothering. About six years later, she decided to take up painting again and began to dedicate her free time to it. She opened a small studio and began to sell her paintings. Because she was now married with family income from her husband's job, she could afford to follow her passion and not compromise her or her family's lifestyle. This compromise worked well for her.

On the other hand, we have all heard the stories of actors, musicians, athletes, and others who sacrificed lifestyle and material things to go after their dream. Jim Carrey lived out of a minivan for a brief time in his life while he was struggling to make it as an actor. Adam Sandler produced his own low-budget films to showcase his talent. He spent several years scraping by, living from paycheck to paycheck to finance these films. He sacrificed his lifestyle because his belief in himself and his desire to "make it" was that strong. These men were so passionate about their craft and so determined to make their dreams a reality that they sacrificed certain things to make their dreams happen as quickly as they could. The unfortunate truth is that with careers like acting or sports, time lines can be an important factor.

Recently, I worked with a twelve-year-old gymnast who

wants to make the Olympic team. He works with a coach five days a week for five hours a day. Finally, he and his family made the decision that he would move across the country to study with an Olympic trainer. This move meant being away from his family and friends and living with a family he didn't know. He was willing to sacrifice his life, as he knew it, his friends, his school, his social life, and his family life, for something he felt passionate about. He knew this was something he just had to do, and that if he didn't, he would regret it. Although being away from his friends and family would be hard, the reward that could come from focusing on his dream full time was worth it. The decision was a tough one, but he made it.

These examples demonstrate the importance of being honest with yourself about what you really want—what is important in the whole picture of your life, now and in the future.

Let's take a look at the categories for determining financial satisfaction.

Be Honest and Realistic About the Things You Want

I remember watching a special about Jane Goodall, the famous scientist who lived in Africa and studied the apes. She has written many books and established several well-known foundations. She has been named Commander of the British Empire by Queen Elizabeth and has received countless awards. For all that glory, I was impressed by what a simple existence she had. She lived in the wild, studied these magnificent animals, and dedicated her life to science and research. Materialistically, she chose to have very little. She just didn't feel the need for much "stuff" out there in the jungle. She certainly didn't need a fancy car because there was nowhere to drive it. She didn't need a beautiful house with great furniture—no one came to visit. And she didn't need fancy clothes—apes aren't impressed with designer labels, and I don't think she was either.

I remember feeling envious of Goodall's lack of need for material possessions. She didn't care about those things. She was on a mission to make a difference. She wanted to educate the world about apes and the environment. She really needed very little. After I watched the program, I thought about how much I enjoy my things. I love having a nice home and a nice car. I enjoy fun clothes and pretty things. Is that wrong or bad? My answer to myself was no. In fact, I have a sense that when I am older, I will want less. I see myself as an older person traveling, studying the meaning of life, and writing about it, as long as David comes along to carry the tent! Seriously, I don't think I will want to be tied to a lot of "stuff." Right now, in my forties with a young family, I like stuff, and that's okay. It's okay to like and want things. It's okay to enjoy fine cars or nice jewelry. Usually, the only people who condemn these things are people who can't afford them.

You were meant to enjoy the fruits of your labor. If you get pleasure from collecting expensive figurines, so be it! This is your life, and you have a right to have the things you want. You just have to be honest with yourself about what they are and then ask yourself what you need financially to get the things you want. Does your career offer you the opportunity to afford the things you want? If not, you need to reevaluate your career and your materialistic desires.

Taking Responsibility for What You Want

Do you secretly expect someone else to get these things for you? This is very common for women who marry with the hope that their materialistic needs met by their husbands. I worked with a young couple named Jordan and Lisa who were married for three years before they figured out that they wanted different things. This scenario is not untypical. She wanted a beautiful home and expensive furniture. She wanted designer clothes and a certain type of car. She was in sales and made a decent salary, but she didn't want to work as hard as she'd have to to get these things. In fact, she didn't really want to work at all. When she met Jordan, she just assumed that he also wanted these things and that he would get them for her. Much to her dismay, he didn't want these things as badly as she did. He didn't care that much about new houses, and he didn't give a hoot about expensive furniture. He was an accountant, and he did fairly well, but he didn't want to work as hard as she wanted him to in order to provide her with these things. He would rather get home early and spend his time working on his car or working around the house.

It was fine for Lisa to want a certain lifestyle and material possessions, but was it fine for her to put pressure on her husband to get them for her? I don't think so. He was making a good living. He was satisfied and living the life he wanted to live. She was the one who wasn't satisfied. She should be the one to do something about it. I know this one is a hard one to 'fess up to, but who says the guy should carry the gal's baggage of desire? I am certain this very issue causes many marital problems, if not divorce. Be honest with yourself and your partner about what you want and how you intend to get it. If you want something, but you're not willing to do the work to have it, maybe it's time to lower your expectations a bit. If you don't, you'll constantly feel shortchanged and dissatisfied. If you're not willing to do the work, you don't want these things as badly as you think you do.

What Kind of Lifestyle Do You Want Now and in the Future?

What kind of money do you need to live the lifestyle you want to live right now? You should be able to live each day the way you want and to have fun every day in some way. You should be able to have a nice home and to decorate it with things you enjoy. You should be able to afford to go out weekly—to movies, to dinner, or to an event with friends—and you shouldn't feel financially stressed about it. You should be comfortable spending money on yourself, especially if you work, and you should allow yourself to do so. You should be enjoying your money and feeling a sense of accomplishment about enjoying it, whether you are buying a new suit, a new book, or a new car. Guilt is not something with which you should constantly be battling when you pull out your wallet.

How much of a role does money play in your daily life? You may think it plays a very small role, but you might be surprised.

From the surface it appears that many wonderful things in my life are free—a warm embrace from my husband, a walk in the snow on a winter night, and sitting in the sun in my living room reading a great book. When you think about it, these things aren't really free at all. Most everything comes with some type of price. If my husband and I were constantly fighting about financial problems, there probably wouldn't be any warm embrace. If we didn't feel good about ourselves by keeping our hair cut, our clothes stylish, and our bodies in shape, we probably wouldn't feel sexy. These things aren't free. And let's talk about that walk in the snow. It takes boots, a coat, and a hat. None of which are free. I live in southern California. To get to the snow, we have to drive or fly, neither of which are free. How about sitting in my living room reading a book. How can that cost anything? Who paid for the house that contains that wonderful sun-filled living room? Who paid for the book? Everything takes work. Nothing comes without a price. You already work for just about everything you get, even affection from your kids. Do you think they would be loving and affectionate if you didn't knock yourself out working to be a good parent? That is part of the payoff—the reward.

Financial satisfaction is about living the lifestyle you want in a way that you can afford. Some of us read books in our living room, some of us fly in our own planes to far away places, and there are a host of lifestyles in between. The key is to begin asking yourself what type of lifestyle you desire now and in the future. What you want for yourself in the future, in retirement, for example, may also affect how you live now.

I know a couple named Mary and Stan who fantasized about having two homes when they retired. They wanted a home in Florida to live in during the winter, and they wanted to keep their home in Ohio to spend summers with their kids and grandchildren. Fortunately, Mary and her husband Stan wanted the same thing, and they began budgeting and saving for it. The only problem was, they didn't quite have enough money to purchase a second home in Florida and maintain the lifestyle they wanted when they lived there. After some planning and discussion, they decided she would get a part-time job, he would still work full time for a few more years, and they would sell their house in Ohio and look for a smaller place or possibly a condo.

Initially, they weren't sure where they wanted to live in Florida. It all sounded like an impossible dream. They decided to take several trips over a few years and to look around at all the various options. The more time they spent there, the more moving to Florida felt like a possibility. They planned and saved and made their dream come true. They knew they didn't want to work when they were there. They knew they wanted to have money to golf, eat out, and live comfortably, and they wanted to buy a boat. They budgeted for all of it, worked hard for several years to save for it, and then they made it their reality.

Establish a Budget and Live Within It

If you constantly feel guilty about spending money, ask yourself, why this is? Do you spend too much? Do you spend money foolishly? Are you financially irresponsible? If your answer is yes, it is time to take financial responsibility for yourself.

One young woman, who went through our outpatient groups for anxiety and depression, loved to watch the shopping channels and loved to spend money. She would buy and buy, and then she would hide her "stuff" and eventually send much of it back. She felt guilty about spending the money because she knew she and her husband didn't have a lot of money to spend. She was a compulsive shopper. She was so miserable, and she was so personally, professionally, and financially frustrated that she took her frustrations out on the shopping channels. This never works. She'd buy fancy things she couldn't really afford, and then she would feel guilty and return them. Through much introspection, she began to realize she needed to change her life. She needed to do something that would make her feel better about herself because no amount of jewelry could improve her self-esteem. In actuality, her irresponsible, spontaneous shopping made her feel worse because it added immense guilt to the picture. She eventually took a part-time job and started managing her money better. She eventually broke her addiction to the shopping channels.

If you feel that you are a responsible person, but you feel guilty about spending money, work on letting go of it—the guilt, I mean. More than likely it is a pattern of behavior pasted onto you from someone else—your parents, maybe. Is it a sign that your chosen profession doesn't support the lifestyle you desire? If this is true, is it possibly time to reevaluate? I believe we need to design a personal lifestyle budget that works for us individually and then stick to it.

For example, our family goes out to eat once a week. David and I go out as a couple once a week. We have an estimated budget in our minds as to what these two nights out will cost us, and we try to stick to it. I have a budget for monthly self-care, such as haircuts and an occasional facial. David works out with a trainer once every two weeks just to keep him motivated and on track. I buy a new suit about once a year, and only buy clothes that work well together and have a sense of timelessness. I would rather buy one really good suit than buy five cheap suits. This works for me because I don't have to wear a suit every day. We budget for two vacations a year, and we have a certain amount allotted for each trip. I don't buy myself jewelry because my husband likes to buy it for me on special occasions. I try to limit going out to lunch to once a week. I'd rather spend money on a chai tea latte every morning. You must know how you like to live and how to budget your money so that you can live this way with confidence and pleasure, without guilt or anxiety.

How Much Money Do You Need to Have to Feel Financially Secure?

The interesting thing about growing up in a lower-middle-class family is that sometimes you don't learn about security, investing in the future, or retirement. I didn't know the value of having money set aside for emergencies. I didn't understand anything about the idea of investing money to make money work for you, and I certainly didn't think about retirement. My family lived paycheck to paycheck. What we had, we spent. If we got more, we spent more. This type of lifestyle offers no sense of security and no sense of responsibility, which are such important attributes to establish when you are growing up.

The Key to Financial Security

We all know people who spend more than they have. They get into terrible debt using credit to purchase things they can't afford. It is so easy to fall into that trap. People end up buying bigger and more because they can go into debt without much thought to whether they really can afford it. I'm not a financial adviser, and I'm not going to give you specifics of budgeting and investing, but I will tell you that it is impossible to feel financially satisfied without doing both. Even if you think you are doing well and can afford to live the way you want, unless you control your money, you will not feel secure. By working within a budget and investing for the future, you take control of your money.

For the longest time, I had a sense that you should enjoy the present and worry about the future later, in the future. I worked hard, I had two jobs when I was sixteen, but I spent all the money I made as soon as I made it. I never saved or invested. I didn't worry about retirement then. I was young! Of course, I didn't worry about it in my twenties either. I lived for the moment. If I hadn't been fortunate enough to have people come into my life to teach me about responsibility, I shudder to think of where I would be right now.

When you budget, you have a sense that you can afford to live the way you want to live, and therefore you can enjoy it. You don't have to worry, because you know you've worked hard, you deserve it, and you can afford it. On the other hand, when you don't work from some type of budget, you are always second-guessing yourself, wondering if you can afford it, worried that you are overspending. Then comes the anxiety and the guilt.

The same holds true for investing. When you put money in investments and watch it grow, it gives you a certain sense of security. You feel that you can enjoy the spending money, the disposable income you have, because you have something to fall back on. You have additional money elsewhere.

As familiar as all this may seem, it is so important in determining your level of financial satisfaction because it all ties together. I know people who are in their forties who don't have money invested or saved. I know people in their fifties who are in debt and unemployed. This is not conducive to a state of financial satisfaction.

A client of mine lost his father, recently, and it was sad to see what had happened to his mother's security. William, my client's father, did well. He was president of a big manufacturing company and made a very good living. They always had beautiful homes, and they even had a beautiful boat. William didn't invest well or manage his money as well as he should have. At the age of fifty-three, he lost his job. He took a few different jobs through the years, he even tried consulting, but his income was never the same. Unfortunately, their lifestyle didn't change to accommodate the change in his salary. Several years passed as they continued to use a good part of their retirement to maintain their lifestyle. And then he died leaving his wife with very little financial security and a house that wasn't paid for.

Financial satisfaction is important to everyone and yet so few people truly feel financially satisfied. If you feel you could be living differently or struggling less, ask yourself what you need to do to change things. Ask yourself if you are willing to do the work to make things better or different. If you aren't, then possibly you need to budget your money differently or get help in putting your finances in order. Financial satisfaction goes hand in hand with financial responsibility, whether you make $20,000 a *year* or $20,000 a *month*.

Operate from an Energy of Abundance

I am a big believer in universal law, cause and effect, and the theory that what you do comes back to you. It is important to operate from the energy of success and abundance. When you do, you will draw money and things that you want to you. If you are constantly in a state of desperation, you create negative energy, and it is harder to get what you want.

Since I created our Attacking Anxiety program fourteen years ago, I have consistently given a lot away—my time, our products, and our services. We never turn down anyone who needs help. We have sent programs to people who are living out of their cars. We offer used programs, loaner programs, scholarship programs, and various low-budget payment plans. I spend a lot of time working with kids for free. For years, my husband complained and said I was foolish. He said it was going to put me out of business and that I was especially foolish to give my time away. But I have seen nothing but positive energy come from it. I really believe it is part of the reason that our company has been so successful. For years, I have watched in amazement as cause and effect have manifested in our lives, and I am happy to say that even David has become a believer. When you put forth good energy, good energy comes back to you.

What can you do to spread some of your wealth around? Can you offer your services for free to someone in need? Can you volunteer and use your talents to make others feel empowered? As I said before, I believe your time is one of your most valuable gifts.

Guidelines for Financial Satisfaction

The guidelines that follow can help you establish a sense of financial responsibility and financial satisfaction.

1. *Be specific and write a paragraph about the "things" you want.* For example, what kind of house do you want to live in: how expensive, how big, location? What kind of car do you want to drive? Specifically, what kind of clothing and miscellaneous

things appeal to you? What other things appeal to you? Make a list of what you'd like. Don't hold back. Do try to stay within your realistic financial potential. Now think about the kind of income you need to afford these things. Is it realistic that you can provide these things for yourself? If not, why not, and what can you do to allow yourself to have them? Begin to see yourself as someone who is worthy and capable of having these material possessions. Change your perception of yourself. Give yourself permission to desire and acquire these things.

2. *Write a detailed paragraph about the kind of lifestyle you want to live from a financial perspective.* How do you want to spend your money on a daily basis? What types of things do you want to do on a less-frequent basis? Possibly you'd like to join a gym or get a weekly massage. Maybe you'd like to eat out more or take more vacations. How would you like to live? Make a realistic budget for this type of lifestyle. Ask yourself how you could allow yourself to achieve this lifestyle.

   How do you want to live when you are older and retired? What kind of money do you need to be able to live that way? What are you doing to ensure that you will have the money you need? Possibly you need to look into a retirement program or talk with an expert about investing. You could attend seminars, take classes, read books, or look to the Internet for advice and direction on how to invest money for the long term.

4. *Begin seeing yourself as someone who enjoys things and give yourself permission to do so.* Everyone likes things of one sort or another. It is okay to enjoy what you have, and it is okay to

work to have more. See yourself as someone who is financially capable, and begin to use your creativity and imagination to think of ways to make money, if more money is what you need. Think out of the box. You can do it!

Financial satisfaction is extremely important in helping a person achieve personal and professional satisfaction, and yet so few people really ever achieve it. For various reasons, people often spend years uncertain of what it is they really want. Once you are clear about what you want for yourself personally, professionally, and materialistically, it is easier to determine what you need to have financially.

I am not saying that you need to have a great deal of money to be happy and satisfied, but it certainly helps. It is possible to be satisfied with very little, but it is a simple fact that money offers us security, freedom, independence, and opportunity. Without it we feel frustrated and insecure. What you need, and what you want for yourself financially, is something you must determine by being honest with yourself.

The following Bill of Rights for financial satisfaction will help you stay motivated to achieve your financial goals:

- You have the right to want and to enjoy money.
- You have the right to enjoy material things.
- You have the right to choose your lifestyle.
- You have the right to a better life.
- You have the right to be anywhere and to fit in anywhere.
- You have the right to feel motivated and driven.

- You have the right to a simple life.
- You have the right to want nice things without feeling guilty.
- You have the right to work hard to have nice things.
- You have the right to feel secure.

Get Creative

There are a million ways to make money. My daughter, Brittany, is always coming up with ways to make money, and some of them are pretty good. One of them was a baby-sitter club in which she would line up girls of different ages for people to employ as baby-sitters. The girls were at different skill levels. The older sitters were more experienced and could stay out late (they were also more expensive). The younger ones were perfect for a day job on a Saturday. Brittany would charge a certain fee and take a cut of each girl's salary. People only had to make one call to get a sitter, and they knew they were going to get a girl who was proven and reliable. People would be willing to pay more because of this.

Sit with your power partner and do some creative brain-storming. What service could you offer that people would be willing to pay for? What could you do to help people and to make money? For example, John comes to my office and home to give me computer support and training for $50 an hour. I don't think he even has a degree, and he probably makes more than most people who do. That's easily $100,000 a year! A woman came to my house to paint a mural on my son's bedroom wall. She charges $300 a day. That's $6,000 a month. There is a guy who comes around our neighborhood and washes cars. I wash my own, but many people use his services. He charges $25 a car and averages three cars an hour. That's $75 an hour. He also details cars for $100 a pop. I am certain he makes well over $100,000 a year. He doesn't work for anyone, and he has a flexible schedule. He loves cars, and he seems to really enjoy what he does.

I know a mild-mannered attorney who probably makes somewhere in the neighborhood of $70,000 a year. He wrote a book last year, a novel, and just recently sold it for $800,000! Of course, this is an extreme example, but anything is possible when you open your mind and allow yourself to dream and then follow that dream.

So what could you do to increase your income level? Anything is possible. What do you want to do? What do you enjoy, and how do you want to spend your time? How much money do you need? Financial satisfaction is possible only when you give yourself permission to want things and then go after them. What are you waiting for?

Part II

CREATING LIFELONG SUCCESS, HAPPINESS, AND WELL-BEING

6

SEVEN SIMPLE STEPS FOR OVERCOMING YOUR FEARS

Needless fear and panic over disease or misfortune that seldom materialize are simply bad habits. By proper ventilation and illumination of the mind, it is possible to cultivate tolerance, poise, and real courage.

— ELIE METCHNIKOFF

From the deck upstairs, I could hear him crying, sobbing really. It was early evening, and my son Sammy, who was six years old at the time, was down the hill playing in his sandbox.

"Don't run down there," David warned. "The doctor said if you do, he'll manipulate you with the same tactics over and over. You can't always go running when you hear him cry." But I was his mother. This was my little boy, and I knew him very well. This cry was different. It was heartbreaking, and in some eerie way, familiar to me, as if I had cried this way myself, many times.

I wandered down the steps toward the sandbox and Sammy. "What's wrong?" I asked, observing my little boy sitting

Indian style in his sandbox with his tear-drenched face in his dirty little hands.

"Mommy, I just want to sit here and play," he sobbed, "and not be afraid."

"Afraid? What are you afraid of," I asked wiping his face with my sleeve.

"I'm afraid that hands will come out of the bushes. I'm afraid of monsters and witches. I heard a noise over there." He cried, pointing to a tree blowing gently in the wind. I brushed my hand through his soft, wind-blown hair in reassurance. He looked up at me, and again he pleaded, " Mommy, I just want to sit here and play and not be afraid."

Suddenly, in that moment I felt his fear, his overwhelming obsession to look over his shoulder because something was "out there," something was going to get him. I understood that feeling. I spent a good part of my life living in fear—afraid of death and dying; afraid of failure and success; afraid of relationships, commitments, people's opinions, not being good enough; and the list goes on.

"It's okay, Sammy." I said in my soothing "mommy" voice. "You just relax and play, and I'll stay here with you. You're safe, and nothing is going to hurt you."

As I sat watching him, I thought how ironic it was that for most of my life I wanted exactly what he wanted. I just wanted to live my daily life and not be afraid. I wanted to stop worrying constantly, stop living in fear of what tomorrow would bring. I wanted to stop my mind from obsessing about everything from illness to embarrassment.

Sometimes it seemed as though my mind was spinning in

endless circles, imagining every possible worst scenario. If the feared situation didn't kill me, the worry surely would. Should I worry about that? I worried about disease, dysfunction, and disaster. Would I get what she got? Did my father's alcoholism ruin my life? Would the world come to an end? I was afraid danger lurked just around the next corner, and as a result I couldn't just relax and play. My fears clouded everything. They kept me from doing things I wanted to do, and even when I did do them, fear was always lurking in the back of my mind.

I watched Sammy let go and lose himself in the moment, soothing himself with gentle humming sounds. I thought about the parallels of this moment and my life. His fears were unrealistic, but then so were most of mine. He needed to trust his surroundings, comfort himself, and stay in the moment. But then so did I.

How many hours, days, and weeks did I ruin in my life, how many vacations or nights out did I destroy because I was worrying about something that never came to be? How many wonderful opportunities did I let pass because I was too exhausted from fear and the insecurity that accompanies it to go after them?

It was interesting to see Sammy relax and trust that I would protect him. He let go and trusted that I would do the "watching out." I would look over his shoulder. He handed all of that fear to me to hold, and he was enjoying the present moment, fully and completely.

Who can do this for me, I thought? *Who can make me feel safe and protected? Who can reassure me, tell me nothing will hurt me, and help me put my worries and fears into a healthy perspective?* I can, and I will . . . and I have. And so can you.

The Fear Response

Fear is a very strong primal emotion. It has a purpose. It alerts us to danger. We've probably all heard the "cave man, saber tooth tiger" story. From the beginning of time our bodies have alerted us to danger, preparing us to either fight or flee.

Our fear tells our body, by means of adrenalin, to run, to fight; to take action. It is quite effective. It is important that you understand exactly what is happening in your body when you put yourself through this fear response, because most of us do this to ourselves on a regular basis with a simple fearful thought. It takes its toll on us emotionally and physically.

Imagine that you are walking out of the grocery store one night. It is dark, and you are alone carrying a bag of groceries. Your arms are full, and you are thinking about how you're going to find your car keys. All of sudden someone rushes up to you and grabs you from behind. You would immediately and automatically go into a flight-or-fight response that would empower you to react and defend yourself. You would feel an immediate rush of adrenalin, and the cycle of automatic reactive response would take place.

The brain alerts the body that danger is imminent. It does this with a thought and then a signal through various neurotransmitters. Immediately, blood transports oxygen and adrenalin throughout the body. As a result, the heart pumps faster and faster. This is called tachycardia, something most people experience when they are anxious. Sometimes they worry that it is a symptom of a heart attack, but it usually isn't.

Next, the adrenalin rushes blood to the large-muscle groups in the shoulders, arms, and legs. These are the muscle groups that need the strength the blood provides because these muscles would be used in battle. The blood is also pushed away from the stomach into these other areas of the body. At this time some people feel nauseated or get an upset stomach and cramping. As this response continues to wreak havoc on your body, your feet or toes might feel numb, in or they might become cold or tingly. The body automatically takes the blood from these areas and moves it into the large-muscle groups because the fingers and toes are more likely to get damaged in a fight. The less blood in these areas, the less blood you are likely to lose. Adrenalin also has the effect of inhibiting feelings of pain. So in the midst of any physically harmful episode, you may not feel the intensity of the pain until it's all over. Isn't it amazing what fine-tuned instruments are bodies are?

When you are afraid, whether from a real danger or from a simple anticipated concern, your muscles are tense and tight. Your breathing becomes shallow. The more you feed the fire with additional fears or worry, the more tension you add. Your body feels like a car in high gear with the breaks on. This is a time when you should get up and do something physical to release the energy caused by the adrenalin, but most people just sit, and stew. Of course, this only adds fuel to the fire.

Adrenalin affects the mind by hyping it all up, turning on all of our alert centers, and we begin to look for danger, imagined or real. The more you worry or focus on your fear, the more confused and bewildered you can feel. People complain of not being able to concentrate or focus. Sometimes all this fear is followed up with feelings of being overwhelmed, eventual exhaustion, and depression. You can experience a sense of hopelessness or doom and gloom.

Your body will restabilize, but it takes time, and you need to let go of the fearful thoughts and go to a place of calm. If you are in a constant state of worry or if you are fearful, you are putting yourself through this horrible response over and over, whether you are sitting on a plane fearful of turbulence or you're sitting at home obsessing about a health problem.

The problem is that most of us alert our bodies when there is no real danger. It is done with a thought. You think you are afraid, therefore you are. You begin to think about something— maybe you are concerned about your health; possibly you are obsessing about a deadline you have to meet; or maybe you are fearful about something concerning your child, your spouse, or your job. What creates the fear doesn't matter. The bodily response is the same—the exact same thing Sammy was feeling. Something "out there" is out of your control and could hurt you in some way. The irony is that most of the damage is caused by your fear.

Fear damages your quality of life. It keeps you from having fun, from doing things you want to do or enjoying them fully. It keeps you from taking risks and trying new things. Fear keeps you from sleeping well, from working productively. It keeps you from living in the present moment. It robs you of intimacy because you are selfishly consumed in your own "what-ifing." It is hard to be there emotionally with or for anyone when you are consumed with concern and fear about yourself and your own life.

For some, fear becomes an excuse. "Maybe I shouldn't take that job. What if I get sick?" "Maybe we shouldn't have a child right now. What if our relationship is unstable? What if *I'm* unstable?" Fear isn't pleasant, but it is very effective when used as a brick wall.

What Are You Afraid Of?

Everyone is afraid of something. I have worked with some very powerful people who have very big fears. One powerful entrepreneur with whom I worked recently has been on the cover of *Time, Business Week,* and *Fortune* magazines. He gives lectures on how to be successful in your own business. He called me concerned about his fear of public speaking! Yet, he does it all the time! "If people knew how afraid I am," he said, "I would feel like a hypocrite. I'm up here telling people to take chances and take risks, and I am afraid to speak. What if I forget what I want to say, or I do something foolish?"

I worked with a rock star who was afraid to fly in his private jet. I worked with a young, healthy, gold cup soccer player who was afraid of dying of a heart attack. I remember a brilliant female stockbroker in New York who feared she was losing her mind.

I know a fifty-year-old powerhouse marketing genius who just lost his job of eighteen years because of corporate downsizing. He is afraid he won't find another one, afraid he won't have enough money to retire the way he wants, afraid he won't have enough money to take care of his family, afraid he looks pitiful in front of his peers, afraid he's too old, and so on and so on.

It is important to try to get to the source of your specific fear. What is the real issue? Do you know what is at the base of your fear?

There's always something to be afraid of, but learning how to control your fear and even use your fear is much more productive than letting your fear control you. As I mentioned earlier, talking about your concerns is helpful, but it's not the complete solution. We must learn to:

Use Fear as Motivation

Here are eight categories that create an operating base for many of our fears. These categories demonstrate the possibility of using our fears in a positive way.

Fear of Loss of Control

According to recent polls, fear of loss of control is the second most common fear about which people complain. Fear of death is third. Believe it or not, fear of speaking in public is number one! Fear of loss of control often co-exists with other fears. In other words, you might fear losing your job, which would create fear of financial destitution and fear of loss of control. If you are the type of person who feels a strong need to be in control of your life and everything in it, fear of loss of control could be a big issue for you. The thought of not being in control of anything in your life can create immense anxiety. Yet real control often comes when we relinquish the need for constant control of everything.

We can't control everything. All we can do is control how we are affected by things. If you are one who fears loss of control, begin now to practice letting go of the need to control everything. Give the reins to someone else once in a while. Delegate, and sit back and relax. The more you practice anything, the better you get at it. Becoming less of a control freak is no exception. Let someone else pick the movie or the vacation spot. Let someone else handle the meeting. You, in particular, need to work on being less affected and more effective when dealing with any difficult or fearful situation. Practice underreacting during those times when things are out of your control. Your real fear is your inability to handle it—fear of loss of control, that is. It is time to prove to yourself that you can.

Fear of Being Alone/Abandonment

Whether you have been with someone for a long time or you have been alone for years, fear of being alone can be ongoing and intense. I believe most people fear being alone. At the core of this fear may lie a deeper fear that I refer to as the "Who will be there for me?" syndrome. What if you would get sick or become dependent in your later years? Who would be there to help you, to sit with you, and to take care of you? If you have ever personally taken care of someone who was sick or dying, you know what I am talking about. It is such a mission of self-sacrifice. Your whole life can get put on hold and turned upside down for an unpredictable amount of time. It is very stressful and a lot to ask of someone. But most people don't ask. They just have someone who loves them, someone who is there and willing to give. Think about this in your own life for a moment. Who would be there for you? Do you have a loved one, a relative, or a good friend? Most of us probably can think of a few people, but if you can't, this is a sure sign that you need to build some intimate, valuable relationships. You must take the time and the effort to build a support system for yourself that makes you feel less alone. If you are retired and even if you aren't, you should look into some of the wonderful new retirement communities available that offer lifestyle diversity as well as assisted living, if it would ever come to that, just so you know what your options are.

I know several older people who have moved to these communities even though they are healthy now and have family support. They've chosen these communities because they don't want to be a burden to anyone should something happen and they want to remain independent. This type of planning ahead involves a mature attitude and a sense of responsibility about your life. I think we will see more of this type of thinking and planning ahead as the baby boomers age and retire.

Alone implies loneliness, emptiness, sadness, and lack of fulfillment. This is what truly scares us. If we look closely at our lives, we find that most of us are alone often, and we handle it well. When we are forced to take care of ourselves, we do. And sometimes we even grow from the experience and enjoy it. Alone then becomes a journey of inner reflection, strength, and self-reliance.

I remember a man who struggled for years with anxiety and mild depression. He avoided many things, from flying to socializing. He had been married for thirty years to a loving wife. He sometimes worried about her dying and leaving him to fend for himself. He just knew he couldn't live without her. She did everything for him. She cooked, she cleaned, and she ran most of his errands. She understood what he wanted sexually and was usually a willing partner. She was a wonderful mother and raised their kids well. She was his enabler. She didn't realize it, and she didn't mean to be, but she was. She did such a good job of taking care of him that he never learned to take care of himself.

To his surprise and everyone else's, she up and left him after the kids were grown! There he was, alone! He couldn't even boil water. He didn't know how to take care of himself in many simple ways because she had done so much for him, from cooking to dealing with the kids' problems to scheduling his doctor appointments. He was thrown out into the deepest depths of the ocean and had to learn to swim.

He was miserable and suffered greatly. His biggest fear, the fear of being alone, had come to fruition. He could remain insecure and dependent and try to find someone else to care for him, or he could take a leap of faith and push himself to grow. Thank goodness he chose the second route.

I am happy to tell you, that after some extremely difficult times and emotional devastation, Mark is a changed man. Not only has he become a gourmet cook, but he is experiencing his children on an emotional level he had never experienced before. Because of his need to get busy learning to be independent, he has overcome his problems with depression and anxiety. He still hopes someday that he and his wife will get back together, but he knows he's safe and capable without her. Even if they do eventually reunite, the change in Mark could only make their relationship more fulfilling.

Use your fear of being alone as motivation to become more independently fulfilled. Get out, take classes, and do whatever it takes to empower yourself. Make more effort to put yourself in situations in which you can make friends. No one can do it for you . . . no one should do it for you. More than likely, we will all be alone sometime in our life, so we'd better be comfortable with the idea. Use any time alone as an opportunity to practice being your own good time and your own source of emotional support. Get out and do things that make you feel more independent and secure within yourself. Ask yourself what scares you most about being alone, and take steps to make yourself feel stronger in that area. For example, if your biggest fear about being alone is loneliness, fill your life with friends or a new hobby. You could take up painting or take a writing class, volunteer, or get a part-time job. Use your fear of being alone as motivation to fulfill your life more, right now.

Fear of Illness and/or Death

This is a big one. Fear of illness and/or death is really fear of the unknown. Many people spend a lifetime worrying about it. In fact, some people are so afraid of dying that they don't allow themselves to live. I mean really live. They don't risk, take chances, or try new things. Use your fear of death as a motivation to live life, every day, to the fullest. Use it to keep yourself forever grateful for the simple things, the things you already have that you can enjoy. You can use your fear of illness as motivation to take care of yourself and to stay healthy. I think it is odd and ironic that many people who come into our clinic worrying about illness or dying smoke and drink too much alcohol and caffeine, or they don't exercise. Use your fear as motivation to get your regular physical and checkups. Afraid they'll find something? Afraid they won't? That's okay and normal. Once you know you're healthy, you can stop worrying . . . at least till your next physical! If you find a problem, early detection is crucial, and recovery and good health are almost always possible these days.

Fear of Embarrassment

No one wants to be embarrassed. Making mistakes or feeling like a failure can embarrass you . . . but only if you let them. The only way to overcome fear of embarrassment is to develop a tougher skin, to reach a point at which you just don't care that much about what others think. Unfortunately, that comes with confidence and self-esteem. If you are lacking in both, this may be difficult for you. First, you need to understand that you are not the center of the universe. Believe it or not, most people are so busy thinking about themselves and their own lives or fears that they aren't thinking about you. Even if you did do something silly or unusual, they would probably forget about it in a short period of time.

I remember a man who had a horrible fear of perspiring in front of people. Of course, his worry caused anxiety, which caused him to perspire. He became so obsessed with this fear that it became difficult for him to socialize or to be involved in meetings at work. At my request, he asked people he knew well if they remembered him perspiring at a particular event at which he remembered that he had perspired profusely. Of course, no one did. I suggested that he talk to himself differently before these events to calm himself down.

He was anticipating perspiring to the degree that he created it. If he could learn to use positive self-talk to change his state, he could control the perspiration to some degree. I suggested he stay away from caffeine, sugar, and other stimulants. Stimulants will cause the adrenalin response, which will cause him to perspire.

Recently, I worked with a very busy professional woman who owned her own business and had an anxious habit of overbreathing. She would breath often and with deep breaths. It sounded as though she was anxious and having a hard time breathing, which was actually happening as a result of her creating it! We decided she could take a breath and cough and then simply tell people she had allergies, which gave her an excuse for the overbreathing. She felt so much better just having an alibi that she barely even needed to use it.

Remember the marketing genius who lost his job through downsizing? He was embarrassed. He felt ashamed, assuming everyone thought he was a failure, which of course no one did. Everyone saw him as a successful, powerful man with many connections and lots of opportunities . . . everyone except for him. Do you think his attitude might affect his ability to land a great new job? I suggested that he needed to stop feeling embarrassed and to start acting as if he was confident and successful. Everyone else saw him as powerful and independent with tons of clout and potential. He needed to start presenting himself that way, to his peers, to his potential employers, and most of all to himself. Of course he felt insecure, but no one else knew he felt that way. A new door was opening in his life, and it was totally up to him and his choice of attitude as to which direction he would take.

Does embarrassment have a purpose? I think we should only feel embarrassed as a form of shame for some type of wrongdoing—if we are rude, if we deliberately offend someone, if we lie, cheat, or do something that is terribly wrong that affects someone else. In other words, feelings of embarrassment should help you to define the boundaries of integrity. Don't ever let fear of embarrassment stop you from taking a risk or from doing something positive in your life. In fact, if fear of embarrassment is a problem for you, I suggest you go ahead and make a fool of yourself. Live, go out on a limb, and act a little crazy. It is okay. It will probably make you more interesting. You will come to realize how little other people's opinions matter.

Fear of Financial Destitution

This fear seems more common to men than to women, but it certainly isn't gender specific. Men tend to worry more about money. Possibly, it is because they feel responsible. They see themselves filling the role of provider, whether they are in this role or not. Many people associate financial security with complete security, personal self-worth, and self-esteem.

Use your fear of financial destitution to motivate yourself to become financially responsible. Start investing and budgeting, as we mentioned in Chapter 5. This will give you a feeling of empowerment and a sense that you are in control. Figure out what you need to feel secure and work on getting it.

Do you need to take a risk and move yourself to a new level? Use your fear of what you *don't* want for yourself (financial insecurity) to motivate yourself to take action to get what you *do* want (financial security). Don't just sit around and worry about not having money. Do something to bring more money into your life. The change in your attitude alone will bring a new energy into your life, which will bring you opportunity. Be open-minded, stay positive, and keep looking for the window instead of the dead-end street.

Fear of Criticism

I used to hate criticism, but now I welcome it. It gives me an opportunity to gain valuable insight about myself that I might not have gotten otherwise. After all, it is up to me whether I pay attention to the criticism. I can ignore it if I want to, or I can analyze it to see if it has any value.

The next time someone criticizes you, pull yourself out of the picture. Pretend for a moment that the criticism is meant for someone else. Listen and don't get defensive, no matter what. Then look at the whole picture and ask yourself what you think. Is there anything valuable in what you heard, anything that you can use? Be an objective listener. You can then thank the criticizer for his or her opinion and move on. I suggest you take some time to think about what was said before you respond. In fact, you don't have to respond at all. It isn't about you . . . remember? It doesn't matter what was said. How you are affected by what was said is the only thing that matters, and that is a choice you make. I suggest you view criticism as an opportunity for growth and enlightenment, period, regardless of the source.

Fear of Losing What You Have

Many successful people are afraid of losing what they have. They finally get the life they want and then ruin it by constantly worrying about losing it. Their worry may manifest as fear of death or fear of some other catastrophe, even fear of financial devastation.

The only good thing about this fear is that it can make you grateful for what you have, though it can make you a prisoner to whatever it is you are afraid of losing, whether another person, a job, or material things.

I remember this happening to a man who lived in Montana on a beautiful ranch. My husband went to college with his son, and we went out to visit them during a holiday. They were heirs to a famous railway magnate. Their private art collection included Renoir, Monet, and several original Winchesters. Their house was magnificent. As wonderful as it all appeared on the surface, there was one catch. This man refused to leave. His wife often traveled, but she went alone. He didn't feel safe leaving all his valuable possessions. He hired people to take care of things for him, but several times items were stolen, or he encountered other problems. He became almost paranoid about being robbed. He had become a prisoner to his possessions. Here was a funny, interesting, worldly man who was living a life of confinement, based on his fear of losing what he had.

Fear of losing what you have, whether it is material possessions, a lifestyle, or a relationship, goes back to the issue of control. The most effective remedy for this fear is to secure what you have as best you can and then forget about it. No one can really be sure about what will happen in the future and what you will lose or gain. The key is to turn your fear of loss into a healthy appreciation of what you have in the present. If you are worrying about losing something, you are not in the present moment. Is living like this worth it? Do you need to reevaluate your priorities, fears, and values?

What good is having a great life if you're constantly fearful of losing it? What good is having wonderful things if you're a prisoner to them? It would be extremely helpful to practice staying in the present moment by focusing on where you are and what you are doing. Give yourself permission to have the things you have, and then give yourself permission and the peace of mind to enjoy them, keeping in mind that they are just things.

Most of your fears probably fit into one or more of these categories. If not, go ahead and create some categories of your own. It is important to know which of these fears keep coming back into your life so that you can deal with them appropriately and work on overcoming them. It is also important to define whether your fear is rational or irrational.

Rational or Irrational Fear

Let's take a look at the difference between rational fear and irrational fear. A *rational fear* operates from the premise that reason and logic constitute the basis for action, or in the case of fear, constitute the basis for concern, which should then lead to action. *Irrational fear* is contrary to reason; it is illogical. In other words, it doesn't make sense to worry about this particular concern because it probably isn't based in reason or reality. The actual chances of the fearful thing happening, although possible, are miniscule.

Let's take fear of flying, for example. Many people who come to our center for help suffer with this particular fear. This fear is a great example of the importance of educating yourself about your concern and gathering reliable information from reliable sources to determine whether your fear is rational.

Often when you are afraid of something, you perceive a danger that really isn't valid. Fear of flying is a perfect illustration. As you've already heard many times, commercial flights are one of the safest methods of travel available today. Yes, there are accidents, and, when they occur they can be devastating. But they are rare. You are twice as likely to die from a bee sting as you are a commercial airline flight. You are 110 times more likely to die on a bicycle. Your chance of death on a commercial airline flight is 1 in 10 million. A sold-out 747 would have to crash every day of the week for ten years with no survivors to equal the highway deaths per year in this country. You are nineteen times safer traveling by commercial plane than by car. Your chances of dying in a tornado is 1 in 150,000, but your chance of dying in a commercial flight is, again, 1 in 10 million!

And how about that turbulence? It may bounce you around and make you anxious, but if you are wearing your seatbelt, it shouldn't physically hurt you. Turbulence is measured in terms of gravity (g) and 4gs of force is considered severe. Today's planes are built to withstand turbulence of up to 8gs. Mother nature probably won't match that, and your commercial flight is programmed to take you around bad weather to avoid the rough air. By the way, there is no such thing as an air pocket and lightning can't penetrate or disable an aircraft in any way. If you are one to obsess about the upkeep and maintenance of the airplane, consider that a commercial aircraft receives twelve hours of maintenance on the ground for every hour it spends in the air. Commercial planes are well equipped with backup systems for virtually every system on the plane. If one fails, the other one will take over. All jets are multiengine. Even three-engine planes can be flown on just one engine. And most planes now have duplicate landing gear and retraction systems. You really do have very little to fear when flying commercially. Therefore, your fear of flying would be considered irrational.

When your fear is irrational, the solution may consist of blocking (stopping yourself from continuing the thought by recognizing that it is irrational) and eliminating the fear. If you determine your fear to be irrational, you need to recognize it and do what it takes to get rid of it. With fear of flying, for example, you might take a fear-of-flying class and then gradually expose yourself to the fear by flying short distances until you get more and more comfortable.

If you determine that your fear is rational, then dealing with it consists of taking action to minimize the fear and taking action to affect the possible anticipated outcome. Simply put, if you determine that your fear is based in logic, you need to take action to do something about it.

Recently a friend of mine called with concern because her teenage daughter had found a small lump under her arm. The mother was understandably concerned. When she felt the lump under her daughter's arm, she said she didn't think it felt like a lymph node. It felt to her like it was in the skin, not under the skin. But to be sure, she took her daughter to a dermatologist. To her surprise he suggested the lump was a lymph node that was enlarged due to an infection. The mother's concern grew stronger. The doctor didn't seem concerned and felt it would "eventually" go away. But the mother had a family history of lymphoma and didn't want to wait and see. She got a second opinion from an internist who confirmed that the lump was absolutely not a lymph node. It was a cyst, as the mother had suspected.

Was the mother's fear rational or irrational? I would say this is a good example of a rational fear, a fear based on information. This fear required a response because it had a logical, reasonable base—her family history of lymphoma. In her search for assurance and additional information, the dermatologist offered a case for more rational concern or fear. She needed more information so she could determine what to do next to take control of the fear.

Secondary Gains

Sometimes we get something out of holding on to our fears. In my "Attacking Anxiety and Depression" program we refer to these as secondary gains. I know that for years I used my anxiety as my excuse "not to": I can't take that new job. What if I get anxious? I can't go back to school. What if I can't sit in the classroom? I can't go on that audition. What if I get sick and make a fool of myself? Sure my anxiety was awful, but at least it was familiar. Taking chances and risking possible failure was unfamiliar. My anxiety was a great avoidance mechanism. It was a real breakthrough for me when I realized that I was using my fear in this way, to avoid things.

What could you be getting out of holding on to some of your fears?

Avoiding Pain: No one enjoys pain. Ending an unhealthy relationship, for example, or quitting a dead-end job could be painful. Even though you know it is something you should do, the pain and the anxiety that it could create may stop you from doing the right thing. Unfortunately the stress of being where you don't belong will cause more pain in the long run. If your fear is related to avoiding pain, ask yourself how much pain and suffering not taking action might create for you.

Avoiding Confrontation: If you have low self-esteem or if you are a people pleaser, you will have a problem with confrontation. You want everyone to like you, to think you are a good, kind, nice person who is in control of yourself at all times. How boring! What successful person do you know who would fit that criterion? Not standing up for yourself or not being assertive is a great way to avoid confrontation and a great way to end up fearful and frustrated. Practice being assertive. It is time to stop running away.

Avoiding Failure: You can't avoid failure, so stop trying to avoid it. We all fail at something. I have failed so many times, and yet I don't think of those times as failure at all anymore. Whatever the situation, I try, I give it all I've got; and if it doesn't work, I just pick myself up, brush myself off, and try, try, again. I learn what I can from the experience and improve from there. As I said in Chapter 2, if you haven't failed much, you haven't risked much. Failure is a natural part of the life experience, and it truly helps to build character, if not a business. Not taking risks, not pushing yourself, avoiding performance on any level, these are examples of letting fear of failure control your life. Recognize it and take hold of it. Push yourself and give yourself permission to fail. It is kind of like flying—the more you do it the less it scares you, and oh the places you can go when you give yourself permission to fly . . . or to fail.

AVOIDING CHANGE: Change is very difficult for most people, although some people thrive on change and the chaos it creates. If you are uncomfortable with change, your fear of change probably keeps you stuck in a comfort zone. Your life may not be what you want, but at least it is familiar. The truth is that change and the vulnerability that comes with it is such a wonderful practice opportunity to use these skills. Change is so growth oriented and fulfilling. If you can step through that wall of anxiety and allow yourself to experience it, the rewards will be many.

AVOIDING WORK: If you overcome your fear and challenge yourself or push yourself, life could demand more effort and more responsibility. You may have to work harder and give up more of your time. Maybe subconsciously you don't really want that, so your fear makes the decision for you. When you get better at defining what you really want for yourself, you will make decisions based in solid self-evaluation and clarity about your personal desires. In turn, you will no longer let fear make your decisions for you.

AVOIDING ANXIETY: When we give our fear power, the fear can keep us from doing things that might make us anxious, for example, flying or speaking in front of others or even changing our lives in some positive way. If we stay fearful, we avoid doing whatever it is we think might create anxiety, and we think again, often subconsciously, that this avoidance will prevent the anxiety. The truth is, not doing the things we want to do will make us more anxious in the long run because we will constantly feel bad about ourselves and our fears. Plus we will feel depressed because we know that we are not living our lives to the fullest.

Facing Your Fears

What are your biggest fears? Now apply the following techniques to gain an understanding of why you have these fears and to help yourself overcome them.

1. Acknowledge what it is that you are afraid of, and accept your feelings of fear. In what category does your fear fit?

2. Ask yourself if you might be using this fear as an excuse not to move forward or to avoid something (the secondary gains we talked about earlier).

3. Educate yourself about whatever you are afraid of so you can judge whether your fear is rational or irrational. Talk to someone who could give you additional information. Get an

expert's opinion. Get on the Internet. Talk with your boss or co-worker. Get more information. Then decide how you can put an end to the irrational fear. If you've had this type of fear off and on for years, there is a good chance it is irrational.

4. If you have a fear of doing a particular activity, let's say flying or speaking in public, expose yourself to the fear gradually, using relaxation and positive self-talk. Set up practice opportunities to work on overcoming this fear by exposing yourself to it and using your new skills. Anticipate positive end results, relax yourself, and talk to yourself in a soothing, comforting manner.

5. Stop scaring yourself with your thoughts, and start empowering yourself with your words. Don't allow yourself to think in self-defeating, overwhelming, fearful ways anymore. We will learn more about this skill in Chapter 8.

6. Give yourself a reward in advance for overcoming your particular fear. If you fear flying, for example, give yourself a special vacation at the end of your fear-of-flying course. If your fear is a health concern, give yourself a special day at a spa once you've gone for your physical. Reward for facing your fear is very important. It is motivation to follow through.

7. Make a strong commitment right now never again to make a decision based solely in fear.

Come to the Edge . . .

Fear is a very powerful emotion that can work for you, as it has for me. I faced my fears, and then I turned my fear into motivation and determination. I didn't want to limit myself or my life anymore. I knew I could do great things if I just stepped out of that comfort zone, if I just pushed myself through that wall of anxiety. You've heard the saying, "Feel the fear and do it anyway." I am a big believer in that philosophy. Nothing is ever as bad as the anticipation of it, and fear is such a horribly consuming emotion. Whatever you continue to fear is something you must work on overcoming because that particular fear is affecting your life in more ways than one. You know this is true.

Be honest with yourself, use your newfound skills, and come to the edge. I think you'll find you can fly . . . in more ways than you ever imagined!

7

WORRY YOUR WAY
TO WEALTH

When you worry, you go over the same ground end-
lessly and come out the same place you started. Thinking, on the other hand, makes progress from one place
to another . . . The problem of life is to change worry
into thinking, and anxiety into creative action.

— HAROLD B. WALKER

Worry—so much of my life was consumed with worry. Why don't I feel good—am I sick? When will I get where I want to be? Did I do the right thing? Why am I not understood, and why can't I be more understanding? When will I achieve what I want, and how do I make the right decisions? How do I accept defeat, overcome my fear, and reestablish my sense of self-worth? What if I don't fit in? What if I never feel fulfilled or content? How do I maintain my faith? Am I good enough for God? What if I end up alone?

I worried a lot about control issues: outcomes, other people, emotions, and situations. I often worried about losing control . . .

of myself, my life, and my sanity. I worried about not being satisfied, about staying motivated, and about how to stop feeling so
angry. I worried about my obsessing. Was I crazy? I even worried about how to stop worrying!

As the years have passed, I've been amazed to find that the
most rewarding experiences in my life have come to me with
very little worry. In fact, many of them have flowed along naturally as if divinely occurring, even when I was worrying desperately about something else happening or not happening. The list
of blessings is long: my husband David coming into my life,
having my children, creating my company and watching it grow,
my writing career, the joy in my everyday life, and my good
friendships.

Life is certainly about challenge, and most things of value
take effort, but we don't have to be struggling constantly. Worry
creates a sense of struggle. Worry and struggle are about swim-
ming upstream against the current with no shoreline in sight.
Worry is about feeling exhausted and overwhelmed and coming
up just short of the brass ring. And yet, worry is a subconscious
choice we make. So why do we choose it? And how can we use
that worry to transform our lives?

What Is Worry?

Have you ever looked up the word *worry* in a dictionary?
The definition is ongoing and overwhelming, filled with
horrific, negative synonymous words and phrases. *Worry* is
defined, among other things, as "persistent torment, torture, the
destroying of one's peace of mind, and (perhaps the most correct

definition of all) overconcern for something impending or anticipated, causing painful mental distress and agitation."

When we worry, we create a mental state of focused concentration, overanalyzing, and anticipation. We use vivid imagination and creative thinking to predict possible horrible scenarios, most of which never come to be. Worry robs us of present-moment happiness, drains our energy, and creates depression and anxiety.

Worry consumes us. It takes over our minds and eventually our moments. It makes us literally sick. We worry to the point of upset stomach, heartburn, and migraines. We let our worry eat at us until finally, in attempt of some relief, we turn to a glass of wine or the latest tranquilizer, all in search of a little peace of mind. We just want to turn it off, but we can't because we don't know how.

Some of us have learned to be worriers. Did your mother worry constantly? Do you have a worry buddy, you know, someone you call when you are scaring yourself to help you decide whether or not you should worry about whatever it is you're worried about? If you think that sentence was intense, imagine what the actual process does to your body! If you are a woman, you probably do have a worry buddy because women worry in groups. They worry with their girlfriends, mothers, and sisters. They affirm each other's need to worry. I think they even enjoy it to some degree. Worrying gives them something to talk about, and most women feel better and are comfortable with sharing their concerns with other women. It is tremendously helpful to talk about your fears and worries.

Men typically worry alone. Often, when their worry does surface, it comes out as irritability, anger, or even depression. It might be difficult for them to put their worries and concerns into words. Men would benefit greatly by talking about their worries with a good male friend or their wife.

Although sharing your worries and concerns is helpful, simply talking about what is bothering you won't stop the problems that chronic worry can create. Constant worry damages your body. You can't put yourself through this stress response again and again and not be affected physically in some way. You may think you are handling things well, but it has to manifest somehow. Possibly you're having some physical symptoms, but you aren't associating them with worry and stress.

I remember a woman named Susan, who worked with me in sales years ago. She was always up and energetic. Her husband lost his job and started having emotional problems. Her mother passed away during this time. Susan seemed to be handling it all quite well. When anyone asked her how she was doing, she said she felt fine and that everything was okay.

One day at lunch, Susan talked to me intimately about a problem she was having that was beginning to concern her. She said she was having muscle twitches all over her body. "You know how it feels when your eye twitches?" she confided. "Well, that is what happens, but it is all over—in my legs, my arms, my lips, everywhere. I get these little twitches. I am scared I have a muscle or neurological disease." I listened, tried to reassure her, and then suggested she go to the doctor to get some resolution. "No! I am afraid he'll find something! I couldn't handle it right now with everything else I am dealing with."

The twitching continued. During this time I watched her go through hell, obsessing that she had a serious illness. After several torturous months of worrying, she finally went to the doctor. The doctor found nothing; the conclusion ... stress. She began to handle things differently. She began to work out, to relax, and to talk more openly about her concerns for her husband. She urged him to get out and have some fun and to stop taking everything so seriously. She convinced him to try a mild antidepressant, and it helped him, along with lifestyle changes. His attitude changed and so did his luck. He got a great job. Coincidence? I don't think so.

Shortly after her diagnosis, Susan's twitching problem began to subside. After her husband started his new job, her symptoms were almost gone. It is amazing what fear and worry and the stress that accompanies them can do to your body.

Stress and anxiety, which are often caused by worry and fear, are associated with heart disease, cancer, stomach problems, migraines, acne, hair loss, and a host of other physical problems. If we learn to control fear and worry, we can improve the quality of our life and provide ourselves with a great dose of preventative medicine in the form of emotional well-being. We can also use the energy and the skill of worry reversal to accomplish our goals.

The Powerful Skill of Worry Reversal

The interesting thing about worry is that it takes certain refined skills. These same skills, when used positively, can help you achieve great things.

We all worry. In fact, some of the most successful and brilliant people of all time were tremendous worriers who used the energy of worry as drive and creativity. Sir Isaac Newton, for example, was often labeled "mad" because of his quirky ways.

Among his personality traits was, of course, worry. He was a hypochondriac, worrying about his health; he worried about fitting in; and he obsessed about sin and death. He used this energy to inspire himself to search for answers and to keep busy. In his search, he discovered many things, including calculus and the laws of mechanics and gravity. His overanalyzing, scrutinizing, and intense intellect were the catalyst for his discoveries. He was one of those people who thought obsessively, but look what it led him to do. He was one of the leading scientists of all time. He became the president of the Royal Society of London and was eventually knighted. And despite his hypochondrias, he lived to the ripe old age of eighty-five.

Sigmund Freud, known as a genius, a revolutionary, and one of the most famous psychiatrists of our time, was full of angst. He obsessed about his sex life, worried about money constantly, was overly concerned with his rivals, and was overly credulous when it came to other medical theories. His own fears and worries, especially those related to his past, led Freud to study human development and eventually to develop his revolutionary theories, including the theory of the subconscious, the Oedipus complex, free association, and dream theory, just to name a few.

These brilliant men didn't know that they were using the energy of worry productively. If they did, they probably would have built a theory around it. Because they are no longer with us, I thought I would give it a try. I call the theory "worry reversal." It is the concept of using the creative energy of worrying to accomplish wonderful things.

It is believed that the average person spends approximately twenty hours a week worrying. Even if you are involved in other physical activities while you are worrying, worry clouds and consumes your thought process, making it almost impossible to function and to think at your fullest creative capacity. What if you took all of your worry time and worry energy and focused it on creating a positive plan of action that could change the course of your life forever? Imagine having an extra twenty hours a week to focus on one specific goal. How much weight could you lose? How could you improve your personal relationships with that kind of focused time? What kind of education could you get, or what kind of business could you build?

Here is the good news. Good worriers make fabulous goal setters and achievers because it takes the same thought processes to worry as it does to succeed: creative thinking, anticipation, analytical processing, and vivid imagination. It is possible to transform the negative energy of worrying into the positive energy of goal setting to create wealth, abundance, and satisfaction in your life.

Let's take a look at how you can use these skills to get what you want.

ANTICIPATION: *Anticipation* simply means you are thinking about what's going to happen, ahead of time. When you worry, you anticipate the worst thing happening. Worry takes a lot of creative energy, and it is exhausting. Negative anticipation is greatly responsible for what I call anticipatory anxiety, when you create anxiety about a situation way before it happens by anticipating it. Often the anticipatory anxiety is worse than the event itself. Fortunately, anticipation is a skill that can work *for* you as well as against you when used properly.

When you set a goal, you also anticipate, but you expect good things to happen. You fantasize about all the possibilities of what you want becoming real. Positive anticipation is exhilarating and energizing—just the opposite of anticipatory worry. You anticipate that what you want will happen and how it will make you feel. You envision how it will change your life.

When we made the decision to move to California, everyone came out of the woodwork to tell us how foolish we were. "It's too expensive. There are earthquakes and fires. You will hate it out there. It is too far away. It's going to fall into the ocean." Can't you just visualize all that catastrophe? I certainly could. But we decided to replace those disasters with thoughts of what *we wanted* to anticipate. We anticipated warm weather, palm trees, opportunities to experience exciting new things, a house near the water. We got what we anticipated.

Anticipate good things and get excited about them. You choose your thoughts, so choose empowering thoughts that motivate you and make you feel as if anything is possible!

Take a moment now and anticipate what you want in your life. Choose one specific goal that you would like to make your reality. Imagine how it would feel to have that goal become real for you. Let your imagination wander as you anticipate the ways this goal could change your life. Anticipation is just the start of believing that you actually can have what you want, whatever it is.

PLANNING: When you worry about something bad happening, you worry about what will happen, how it will happen, how it will feel, and what you need to do to prevent it. When you set a goal, you think about what will happen, how you can make it happen, how it will feel when it does happen, and what you need to do to make it happen. You see the thought parallels here? One will make you sick, the other will make you successful.

You need a plan of action to make anything happen. Do you know people who are already doing what you want to do? When can you talk to them? What advice can they give you? How much money do you need to achieve your goal? What kind of time frame are you working with? Whom do you need on your team? Friends who support and believe in you? Do you need additional employees or investors? What is your plan of action? What are your action assignments for yourself? Do you need to schedule a meeting or make some phone calls? If you are busy planning for your dreams, you won't have time to worry about the stupid things.

Now, take a few minutes to jot down some notes about how you could devise a plan of action to bring your goal that much closer.

ANALYZING: When you worry, you examine the possibilities and the details of the anticipated concern. This is where you can get into trouble. If you are a worrier, you probably analyze things to the last detail. Why is this happening to me? What do I do? Why did he say that and what does it mean? When you use this "skill"—and, yes, it is a skill—in positive pursuit of a goal, you can establish a good case for your goals becoming a reality: Of course achieving the goal is a possibility, and here is why. Of course there are options, and here's what they are. I can absolutely make it happen, and this is how. See the difference?

When you analyze your goal, you think of all the options, all the ways you can make it work. You must get specific. There are always a hundred different ways to look at things. Get more information. Go to the library and get on the computer. Find a mentor. Know the best direction for you to take and know why. There is always a way.

I remember when my company was very small, and we needed to find a better distribution channel for our "Attacking Anxiety" product. We saw all these infomercials for self-help items, and we thought, "Hey, our product could sell on an infomercial and, what a great way to educate the public about anxiety disorder." Tony Robbins was very big at the time, so we called the company that produced his show. They weren't interested. They said our market was too narrow. I was convinced it would work on an infomercial. The product was wonderful, and best of all it really worked. We had thousands of wonderful testimonials. There had to be someone who would take a chance on us. We tried everyone. No one was remotely interested.

I knew if we didn't do something to diversify distribution, we would not be able to survive. We gave too much away. We were understaffed. We had to do something. We had to take a chance on what we believed in, our product. We decided to produce an infomercial ourselves. My brother Michael and I went out and hired two camera guys and a makeup person. I sat and interviewed real, warm, and sincere people who had changed their lives as a result of using our tape program. We edited the show on our home VCR.

I'll never forget when we sat in our tiny little office watching our infomercial air on a local television channel. We were so proud. We hired a couple of grocery store clerks from my husband's family grocery store across the street to help answer the phones. We were shocked and amazed when the phones actually rang. It worked! Thank God, we didn't give up when we were told it wouldn't work. After years of dedication and persistence, that infomercial is the number one self-help infomercial in the world today.

Get a pencil, and write down at least ten different ways you could make your dream come true. Think hard. What are your different options? What are your plans B, C, D, E, F, and G? Don't let anyone tell you it won't work or that it can't be done. It can! How bad do you want it?

CREATIVITY AND VISUALIZATION: This is one of my favorite skills—making it real and seeing it in your mind. When we worry, boy can we get creative! Examples would be the man who worries about his health and actually imagines dying in some horrible torturous way; or the women who worries about her husband having an affair and actually pictures him in the arms of his co-worker; or the mother who worries about her teenager getting in a car accident and actually visualizes the crash and her son on the side of the road. Yuck. We have all done it, though. We have all made ourselves "sick" with this "skill."

When you use this creativity and visualization to set a goal, it doesn't make you feel bad or frightened or worrisome. It makes you feel energized and empowered. You must brainstorm about all the creative things you can do to make your goal a reality. You visualize yourself walking on that campus to get that degree. You see yourself twenty pounds thinner wearing that fabulous new bikini. You vividly imagine yourself in that brand new sports car—you know, the one you've wanted all your life, the one you're supposed to drive to your twentieth class reunion. It's red, and it's a convertible. See how it works?

Just recently I came across an article I had written more than ten years ago about creativity and visualization, and in it I described a certain type of house I wanted to own some day. I had forgotten about that article. I was intrigued when I read it to find that I am living in the exact house I described at that time, right down to the type of doors in the living room, the age my kids would be when I lived there, and the view out the back door. It was almost spooky to read it, and it certainly validates everything I am saying here.

Let your imagination run on this one. Get specific. Right down to the color of the car, or the location of your dream home, or the type of person you are thinking you want to spend your life with. I will really get specific about the technique of visualization in Chapter 10. Visualizing what you want is a very important part of the process of getting it.

DESIRED OUTCOME: When you worry, your desired outcome is that the negative thing you are worried about *won't* happen. But have you ever noticed how worrying about something doesn't prevent it? I think some people believe worrying about a situation gives them a sense that they are doing something about it. But worry is not pro-active, it is re-active. Worrying doesn't make something happen (except, of course, the stress response); it is the result of something happening (your anticipation and thoughts).

When you set a goal, you also have a desired outcome—that what you are striving for will become a reality. When you define what you truly want, overcome your fears, transform your worry into goal setting, and keep yourself focused on your desired outcome, you will make it happen. It is cause and effect. It creates a sense of synchronicity, which we will also be discussing in detail in Chapter 10.

Don't focus on what you don't want. Focus on what you *do* want! Doesn't that make sense? What do you want so badly that you can taste it? What brings you joy when you imagine it coming into your life? Allow yourself to daydream and fantasize, and go for the gold.

The idea here is to block your negative and worrisome thoughts when you begin to get into a worry mode and then to replace them with something productive. Use your time productively to work on a plan of action to get what you want. Push your worries out of your mind and don't allow yourself to worry at any time except for your planned worry time.

Planned Worry Time

How do you deal with all the worries and concerns that bombard you throughout the day? Many of our group participants have had great results with a technique I call "planned worry time." It is my Scarlet O'Hara theory—you know the one, "I'll think about it tomorrow." Well, you'll think about it later. Set aside a time of day, preferably early evening, to assess all your worries from that particular day. For example, you will worry about anything and everything that comes into your mind space today at 7:30 P.M. So, until 7:30, you will not think about any spontaneous or reoccurring worry that creeps into your mind in any negative worrisome way. You will simply say to yourself, *I'll think about it tonight, during my planned worry time.* You stop the thought and then replace it with something that helps you see the worry as an opportunity to solve the problem. This is the technique referred to earlier as "blocking." (This would also be a good time to practice the diaphragmatic breathing you'll be reading about later in this chapter.)

What often happens when you push your worries out of your mind, not allowing yourself to dwell on them, is that you forget half the things you were going to worry about. It is an automatic process of elimination. Also, you will begin to use your worry time to problem solve, to take action to minimize or to eliminate the problem.

When you find yourself drifting into a worry mode, it is time to get pro-active. Practice your breathing and use empowering self-talk to calm yourself. Then, make a list of your top three concerns. Under each, ask yourself how you could take control of this concern by using some of the skills in this book. What action could you take, based on what you are learning here, to alleviate your fear or to create a workable solution? If you can't come up with a solution to the problem, it may mean that your fear or concern is irrational. Most *rational* fears have a solution in the form of getting more information or taking some type of action.

During your planned worry time, go ahead and worry. But at the end of your worry time, make a few notes on how you will be dealing with each issue and put a time line on each. Then put your notepad aside until your next worry session.

Underreacting and Time-Out

Sometimes there just doesn't seem to be an answer or a solution to a problem. Sometimes you just feel too tired to deal with things. This is a good time to practice underreacting. To do this, ask yourself how you could respond with less effort, less energy. Possibly respond just the opposite of what you would normally do. Don't call your worry buddy; take a bath instead. Don't sit and fret; go out for ice cream or a nice dinner. Don't run to the medical book; get up and go work out. Don't reach for that glass of wine; go make love to your spouse!

Another effective technique is to take a time-out. Don't deal with the worry for twenty-four to forty-eight hours. Then revisit the issue. You will find if you were angry, your anger has become defused. If you were worried, you probably have some solutions or a better perspective. Take time and don't respond immediately. If you do respond immediately, there is a good chance that you will do what you've always done, which hasn't worked so far, or that you will overreact, which will just create more anxiety.

Worry is a bad habit you've gotten into. You need to begin retraining your pattern of thinking and your automatic response to that type of thinking, so that it is pro-active instead of re-active.

The minute you begin to worry, ask yourself, "What can I do to solve this?"

Do I need to get more information?
Do I need to take some kind of action?
Do I need to underreact?
Do I need to take a time-out?
Do I need to realize that this fear or worry is irrational and use positive thought replacement to defuse it?

These are your choices. I guarantee you that using one of these options will help you to feel that you have a sense of control over your worry and fear.

Medication for Chronic Obsessive Worrying

I specialize in working with people to help them overcome problems with anxiety and depression. Most of their problems are worry induced. People worry about dying, about losing their minds, about embarrassing themselves, and so forth. When someone is consumed with worry, he or she is depressd and disempowered. Worrying takes so much energy and thought process. Chronic worry can create severe anxiety, panic attacks, and various levels of depression.

Is there a pattern of worry that seems to haunt you? Do you constantly worry about the same types of things? Could you have a problem with obsessive thinking? If you do have an ongoing problem with constant obsessive thoughts, talk with your doctor. There are many medications that can be helpful in stopping this torturous experience. If you are obsessing constantly, it is torturous and unnecessary. Talk with your doctor about the positive effects of such mild medications as Prozac or Celexa for helping you to take control of this problem.

Breathe Your Worry Away

When we worry, we increase our breathing rate or overbreathe, as we talked about earlier. Unknowingly, we may be chronically hyperventilating. Most people think of hyperventilation as panting or gasping for air, but other forms would include yawning, sighing, or taking a deep breath. When we hyperventilate in any way, we alter our body's biochemistry, changing the balance of our body's level of carbon dioxide, oxygen, and adrenalin.

This chemical reaction caused by overbreathing can create additional symptoms, including dizziness, faintness, feelings of bewilderment and confusion, and shortness of breath. These symptoms actually cause us to worry and to be even more afraid. First, we worry about whatever our particular concern is. Then we overbreathe. Then chemicals released into the body create more symptoms. Then we get anxious.

Understanding this cycle is very important because, if you learn to pace and slow your breathing, you can learn to control and ease your feelings of fear and worry. In fact, it is proven that if you take control of your breathing and begin to slow it down at the onset of worry, you will minimize the worry. You can actually prevent yourself from going into an obsessive worry overload.

Breathing in a controlled, paced fashion is a form of breathing referred to as diaphragmatic breathing. In other words, you are breathing from your diaphragm, not your chest. When you breathe from your chest, you increase your chances of hyperventilation.

I strongly suggest you practice the following technique three times a day for two weeks until it becomes second nature to you. Once you have mastered the skill of paced diaphragmatic breathing, you can call on it whenever you feel yourself going into worry mode. You can do it while standing, sitting, or lying down.

To practice this exercise for the first time, I suggest you lie on the floor with a small object, such as a small pillow or stuffed animal, placed directly on your abdomen, the area about one inch above your navel, just below your rib cage. Your goal is to breath from this area. Your diaphragm is the muscle underneath the lungs. When you breath in, your diaphragm and abdomen area should push out, moving the pillow up. When you breathe out, the diaphragm and abdomen should be sucked in, causing the pillow to sink in. As you breathe in, the pillow and your abdomen will rise; as you breathe out it will sink back in.

Practice this movement for a few minutes. Next, try to focus on your breathing, keeping it at a smooth, relaxed pace. It may help to breathe through your nose, because breathing through your nose usually forces you to breathe more slowly. Next try to pace your breathing to twelve breaths per minute. This means you will breathe in and immediately breathe out, at five-second intervals. You will breathe in and then breathe out, and then wait to breathe again for five seconds. This may be difficult to do at first, but it will get easier the more you practice. The more you practice this exercise, the better you will understand how important is to pace and slow your breathing when attempting to control your worry and fear.

Wealth Is So Much More Than Money

When I talk about worrying your way to wealth, I am talking about using the skills of worry to achieve abundance in all areas of your life. Wealth is so much more than money. Consider abundance, well-being, fulfillment, and contentment. You are also wealthy if you have good health and peace of mind. How many of us can say we have achieved all of that? Very few, I am certain. And I am also certain that our worry and fear keep us from achieving these things.

Worry can be a ticking time bomb, waiting for the right moment to explode. Worry can be a weight that we carry on our backs and shoulders, adding a sense of heaviness to everything we do and want, or it can be a dark cloud that follows us around, constantly threatening to rain on our parade. Worry can be a nagging, familiar, irritating "friend" in our life, someone we'd like to get rid of but aren't sure how to do it. Besides, with whom would we replace that friend? Maybe we don't like this person, but at least it is some form of stimulus. How about replacing that negative stimulus with possibility thinking?

Thinking from *It Not* of *It*

A friend of mine named John was the producer on an audio program I created a few years ago. I remember a particular day when John and I met in the lobby of a hotel in Los Angeles to discuss the product. Since we both play guitar and write music, John decided to bring his beautiful acoustic guitar with him. We laughed, talked, and even played guitar and sang a bit. It was a great afternoon. I was scheduled to do a seminar that night, and John was going to play guitar at the event. We headed out to get our cars.

Later that evening at the seminar, I caught up with John again, and he had some disturbing news. He told me that when he got in his car, he forgot to pick up his guitar. He had accidentally left it out in the street in the hotel parking lot. He didn't realize it until later that night when he went to get the guitar for the seminar and didn't have it. I knew how expensive his guitar was, and how much it meant to him. He was an entertainer and played often. He had had this guitar for quite some time. This was Los Angeles. That guitar was history.

"I'm so sorry, John," I said. "I know how much that guitar meant to you."

John looked at me and said, "No, I'll get my guitar back."

"How are you going to do that?" I asked, puzzled by his confident attitude.

"I'm going to think *from* it, not *of* it. It is a theory described by a philosopher named Aaron Neville. It's simple. Instead of thinking, 'Gee I hope I get my guitar back. What if I don't? Who would turn it in? What are the chances in L.A.?' I'm thinking, 'That guitar belongs to me. It's mine. I own it. I already have it.' Think *from it*, 'It is already mine.' Don't think *of it*, 'It could be mine.' Do you see the difference?"

Instead of worrying about all the reasons why he might never get the guitar back, John used his worry energy to think of all the reasons it was already his and that it was already back. This is very powerful universal energy to put "out there" where energy creates action.

What do you think happened? The next day he got a call from the hotel. Someone had turned in his guitar. I have to admit, I was pretty amazed. John was validated.

As I thought back on my own life, I have spent much of my career teaching this same type of philosophy. Think about what you want, and believe that you can have it. Nevel just takes it one step further: Believe that it is already yours. The point is that if you are going to expend this energy anyway, why not use it productively?

How do you know when your worry energy is going in the right direction? You will feel hopeful. If you are going in the wrong direction, you will feel hope-less. The next few chapters will help you greatly in choosing the right words, phrases, and thoughts to keep your energy positively focused.

Positive Addiction

Worry is a bad habit. It is something you have learned to do and practiced daily. The wonderful thing about the negative and addictive thinking pattern of worry is that it can almost always be turned around and stabilized into the positive addiction of goal setting and taking action in some way. One is harmful, the other is healthy and productive.

Remember to:

Anticipate positive results.
Plan for success.
Analyze the possibilities.
Focus on the desired outcome.

Also . . .

Set up a daily worry time.
Block your negative worrisome thoughts.
Practice your diaphragmatic breathing.
Replace your negative thoughts with comforting, calming, empowering, problem-solving self-talk.

How much time have you wasted worrying about not getting what you want? How creative are you at coming up with all the reasons why what you don't want could happen? You choose to think this way. Wouldn't it be more healthful and more productive to choose to use your worry energy in positive pursuit of a dream?

The choice is yours. At least now, you know you have one!

8

POSITIVE, PRODUCTIVE, POWER THINKING

The deepest principle in human nature is the craving
to be appreciated.

— WILLIAM JAMES

You're beautiful. You're exceptional in so many ways. You are a piece of work. You are an incredible work of art. Your face, your eyes, everything about you is embraceable. You are someone people want to be with. Time spent with you is a pleasant and memorable experience. You make the world a better place. You make the word *love* easy to understand. You put out good energy. You are capable of great things, and you are full of spirit. You are a breath of fresh air, a beautiful flower opening to the warmth of the sun. You make me want to dance, to laugh, and to play. Your eyes sparkle. I know I am safe with you, everyone is; you are a good soul. I like to watch you—you are a great play, an opera, a picture on canvas. You have such a story to tell, and I love to just listen. You are full of intense emotion. You are alive and living with gusto. I want to walk with you, to hear your stories. I want to share your pain and wipe away your tears. I want to be your friend. You are valuable, worthy, and unique. You are a gift from God. We all are.

As you read the previous paragraph, to whom did you think it was referring? Did you think I was writing to or about one of my children or possibly my husband? As you read it, did you find yourself wanting to be admired and cherished in this way? Did you wonder if I might possibly be talking to you?

When I had finished this chapter and read the first paragraph out loud to my daughter, Brittany, she asked me if it was about her. She seemed confident that it was. It made me feel good to think that she felt she fit the description, that she sees herself as this type of person, and that she knows that I would describe her in this way.

The truth is that as I wrote that paragraph, I thought about all the people in my life whom I cherish. My children, my husband, my mother, my brothers and their wives, my nieces and my nephews, my girlfriends, my son's teacher, my daughter's best friend, my son's drum teacher, my dearest friend from work, and many others. I have sat in cars at my son's school and cried with mothers of sensitive children. I have sat in coffee shops with smart women friends and listened as they shared their insecurities. On a flight from Detroit to Los Angles, I have sat beside an amazing man who was dying of cancer and coming out to see his children one last time. These are all very special people to me.

I am in awe of people. We are all so tender. We need each other. We need to know that we are going to be okay; that we are okay.

We have all been given an incredible gift that holds the power to make others feel better, good, safe, loved, secure, understood, strong, capable, and the list goes on. It's the gift of conversation.

What we say and how we say it. What we say is truly one of the most intimate, quickly devoured, and acutely acknowledged sources of communication, and yet we abuse it all too often.

Are you aware that you can change someone's mood, possibly one's entire day, or even entire life, by saying certain things? So why do we hold back from giving this most precious and powerful of all gifts?

The Call for Compassion

The world is a tough place. It is full of busyness. It spins around us offering very little in the way of security and validation for just being who we are. In fact, the world as we know it seems to offer validation for just the opposite. Who we are isn't good enough anymore. We should be prettier, thinner, flashier, smarter, more successful. We should have whiter teeth, bigger breasts, and flatter tummies. We should never look old and never be depressed, or, if we are, we certainly shouldn't talk about it.

God forbid you don't fit into the mold, even at an early age. I watch in horror as kids with various challenges, from attention deficit hyperactivity disorder (ADHD) to depression to dyslexia, struggle in school to fit into a system that has no place for those who march to a different drummer. I watch in disbelief as people judge these children because they act differently.

If you have been with a child who isn't quite like the others, a child who is challenged for one reason or another, you know what I am talking about. It is amazing what loving, inspirational words can do for a sensitive child. A gentle hand, a smile, a positive compliment to the child, and a look that says, "Hey, you're okay, you're loved" can make such a difference to that child. I have seen the power of this kind of input over and over again . . . and not just with children. Adults crave it as well. We all need validation that we are loved and capable.

Being a Compassionate Person

One of the most beautiful characteristics of my fourteen-year-old daughter, Brittany, is that she is a compassionate person. I hear her with her friends telling them how special they are. She is so good at making someone feel better. Her voice is soothing; her words are confident and reassuring, as she uses well-chosen words to talk someone through a difficult situation. She has learned the art of compassionate conversation. This will come in handy as she falls in love, chooses a mate, pursues a career, and becomes a mother. All of these situations, if they are paths she chooses, will call for compassion.

How do we learn the art of being compassionate? Not surprisingly, the people who are best at being compassionate to others are usually people who are good at being compassionate to themselves. Someone who talks to himself or herself lovingly will be good at talking to others in this way. And the opposite is true as well. A person who beats himself up verbally usually tends to be more negative with others.

I say usually because sometimes people who are highly critical of themselves are very sensitive with others. They understand pain and are sensitive to other people's pain because they themselves experience it often, as a result of their low self-esteem.

A woman I have known socially for quite some time is one of the kindest people I have ever met. She is giving and does so much for others in need. Even though she is giving and loving to others, I have always sensed a certain passive, low self-esteem. She is always saying good things to and about other people, yet she doesn't say good things about herself. Recently she shared with me that she was sexually abused at a young age. As a result she understands pain and fear and can be sensitive and supportive to someone else. Yet, she is incapable of being loving to herself. I pointed this out to her and suggested she work with a rape therapist to learn how to get beyond the pain and to begin to nurture herself.

Are You Compassionate?

Ask yourself the following questions and answer them honestly:

Do I tend to see the negative side of a situation?

Do I find fault easily?

Do I enjoy putting others in their place?

Do I get uncomfortable when someone expresses painful emotions to me?

Am I at a loss for words in a difficult situation?

Do I complain often to others or to myself?

Do I have friends who are negative?

Do I often feel misunderstood?

Do I sometimes "jokingly" make fun of others?

Do I feel uncomfortable around someone who is challenged or different?

Am I judgmental?

Do others accuse me of being insensitive?

If you answered yes to two or more of these questions, you might be lacking in the skill of compassion. Obviously, the more yes answers you have, the more you need to work on being more positive with others. If you did answer yes to several of these questions, it could be why you don't have many good friends or why you have a hard time with intimate relationships. Possibly this is part of the reason for your family problems or even marital problems. It could be part of the reason you have problems at work or trouble communicating with your children. This is a skill that you need to learn. It will make you a better friend, lover, and parent. It is such a horrible feeling to pour your heart out to someone and then have him or her be nonresponsive or, even worse, cynical or sarcastic. It is almost impossible to build an intimate relationship with someone who does not have a compassionate heart or an ability to express compassion verbally.

When we first moved to California, we were trying to adjust to the move and the new environment. We didn't know anyone or have any relatives in California. Several months passed, and the kids were making new friends and fitting in beautifully. I wanted a good friend. I met a woman in the community whom, initially, I really liked. She was interesting, smart, and had a quirky sense of humor, and we seemed to have several common interests.

We began to do a few things together with the kids and also by ourselves.

As time passed and I spent more time with her, I began to see a cynical side to her. She was sarcastic and brash at times, and it was difficult for her to be sensitive to anyone who needed compassion, even her own children or other family members. As time went on, I recognized more and more signs that this was not an emotionally sensitive woman or a very happy person.

My husband didn't care for her from the beginning. He said he thought she seemed selfish, self-centered, and cynical. He was right, but it took me longer to see it. I tried to talk with her about it a few times, but she wasn't ready to hear it. I evaluated the situation, pulled back, and ended the friendship.

The sad thing is that I have noticed that this woman has a hard time keeping friends. She also has very strained personal relationships. I am certain it is because of her inability to be compassionate and to communicate in a positive, loving, supportive way. On the surface, she is great, but intimately she is deficient. She is critical, judgmental, and insensitive.

If you recognize yourself as someone who has a hard time with the skill of compassion, and you want to change, this is good place to start. If you feel that you are compassionate to others, but you need work on being more compassionate to yourself, then this chapter is for you as well. Learning to be a compassionate conversationalist begins with you and how you talk to yourself.

Self-Talk:
The Key to Healthy Self-Esteem

As I said earlier, people who are good at being positive and compassionate with others, people who are good at being cheerleaders, of sorts, are typically good at being compassionate and motivating to themselves. If you aren't good to yourself, if you are negative, worrisome, and full of angst, you probably don't have the patience, self-esteem, or skills to be emotionally supportive of others.

Thinking negatively is a bad habit. It is something you have learned to do with years of practice, and it comes naturally to you.

Don't feel bad. Thinking negatively comes naturally to most people, even those of us who believe ourselves to be positive thinkers.

And why wouldn't it? We are bombarded with negative messages every day. The media is full of negativity. Violence and vulgarity is everywhere if you simply turn on the television or the computer.

The average person has over 250 negative thoughts a day. That calculates out to a person virtually beating himself up verbally about once every two and a half minutes. Think about it. " I don't feel good. I feel fat. I don't want to go to work today. Oh crap, it's raining. I'm tired." There are five negative thoughts! How long do you think it would take to get to 250? You are probably more negative than you realize.

When I work with people who struggle with panic, anxiety, and depression, the first thing I must do is convince them that they are thinking in a negative way that actually creates their anxiety and depression. I say "convince them," because most people believe they are positive thinkers. They think that they have healthy attitudes and that other people who are negative cause most of their problems.

When I say "Thinking negatively is a bad habit," I mean it is similar to the bad habit of being angry. The more you practice anything, the better you get at it, whether it is being angry or thinking negatively. Whatever you tend to do naturally is what keeps resurfacing time and time again, whether it works or not. The problem is that most of us don't realize these types of negative traits as bad habits, as things that can be changed and overcome. Instead, we just accept that this way of thinking is who we are. We don't realize that we are negative thinkers, and we don't realize how much that state affects our attitudes and, consequently, our lives.

When you become a positive, productive, power thinker, other people can't cause problems for you as easily because you use positive self-talk to be less affected by them. You are strong within yourself about who you are and compassionate with yourself about what you are feeling as a result of something that happened outside of you.

What is positive, productive, power thinking? It is just that . . . power. You can reassure yourself, motivate yourself, calm yourself, relax yourself, comfort yourself, and empower yourself. You can be more effective when there are things you want to achieve and less affected when there are things you don't like happening around you. You have the power inside you. No one can hurt you because you know you will be okay no matter what the outcome, because you can take care of yourself emotionally. You can make yourself feel better.

The POWER in Positive Self-Talk

A client of mine named Diana, who is an author, was recently asked to appear on a very big national talk show. She was told she would be given the full hour to talk about her book and share her skills. She works with people with disabilities. As is typical with talk shows, the producer asked her to provide guests who had disabilities to appear with her on the show. She brought in several very special people from all over the country who were willing to share their stories.

When she arrived at the show, people were treated abruptly, and everything was moving very quickly. Two minutes from taping the show, the producer informed Diana that where she would be seated during the show had changed. Originally, it was agreed upon that Diana would be on the stage with her clients throughout the entire show. Now the producer was saying the host wanted Diana placed in the front row of the audience, offstage. Diana had worked with me on self-esteem and positive power self-talk for several weeks. As a result, she had become quite comfortable with being assertive and confident. She simply replied that sitting in the audience was not acceptable and not what she had agreed to do.

There was an immediate uproar. Within minutes she was standing in the green room with the very powerful host trying to intimidate her. "Let me make something clear to you. This is my show," she said with attitude, her finger pointing in her face. "You do it my way or not at all!" Diana stood firm and didn't flinch. "I am responsible for these people. If your producer had told me I was not going to be on stage, I never would have agreed to do this show," she said with cool confidence. "That's it!" the host screamed. "This show is canceled!" and she ran out the door.

Now consider for a moment that Diana had brought seven sensitive people to do the show, people who had flown in from around the country and who had various disabilities to deal with. Diana had spent weeks preparing for the show, and she also had flown six hours to be there. Was the host thinking about any of them? Of course not! Welcome to the real world.

Diana explained to me that she stood there completely in control and thought about her options. She said, "Within seconds

I felt myself taking control. I told myself that I was okay, and that this host was trying to intimidate me. I reassured myself that she could not hurt me or negatively affect my life in any-way. I had the power. I had made up my mind that if the show were cancelled, I would take my clients to lunch and have a wonderful time with them. We all had a free trip to New York. No great loss. This host had no power over me."

The host couldn't hurt her or intimidate her because Diana wouldn't let her. She just kept putting it back on the host in her mind. She thought to herself, *What is her problem? She is really stressed out. She must be insecure and a power maniac. She cannot hurt me. I'll just walk away and go take these people to lunch. It isn't the end of my world, or theirs, not to do this show.* Do you see the power this gave her, the feeling of control? This is where true personal power comes from.

An amazing thing happened. The host, who is known by her producers as a difficult, controlling person, came back and nego-tiated. As a result of Diana's standing firm and being confident, she respected her, and the show went on. Diana was brought up on stage. The host did a wonderful show and treated both Diana and her guests with respect.

Diana said that before she learned these skills, she would have been extremely intimidated by this woman. She would have given in out of fear and frustration. But she now had feel-ings of power and self-confidence. A feeling that the host couldn't "hurt" her or take away her power. She stood up for herself and stayed cool. Most important, it was the messages she gave herself, the way she talked to herself, telling herself that she would be okay, no matter what the outcome, because she was in control of how she handled it. The host could control the situation, but only Diana could control how it affected her. She chose not to be affected. This is complete and total power.

Becoming a Positive, Productive, POWER Thinker

How do we become positive power thinkers? You must admit that you think negatively and that it is getting in your way. This is half the battle. This is why Step 1 in the following exercise, which refers to writing down your negative thoughts, is so important. By tracking your negative thoughts, it will become very clear by the end of the week that you are sabotaging some of your potential for success and contentment.

The skill of positive power thinking, like any other skill, has to be learned and then practiced, practiced, and practiced. And like most new skills, it gets easier the more you practice it.

STEP 1: *For one week, carry a small pad of paper with you, and jot down every negative thought you have*, from "I'm tired," to "I feel like a bad mother," to "I feel fat," to "I feel like such a hypocrite." You might need a pad for every day depending on how many negative thoughts you have! Be sure to write down any thought that makes you feel bad, sad, unattractive, tired, unmotivated, week, insecure, depressed, overwhelmed, unloved, angry, annoyed, or any other negative emotion or feeling. This may be hard at first because you will be looking for them. If you are consciously waiting for yourself to think negatively, you aren't as likely to do it. In fact, you'll probably subconsciously attempt to think more positively to prove to yourself that you are not a negative thinker. Eventually, you will relax and get back to your old way of thinking. This is why I suggest you do this exercise for at least one week.

STEP 2: *Try to write positive replacement thoughts for the negative thoughts you wrote down.* In other words, write another statement or group of sentences to replace the negative ones that relate to the same issue. Make sure these are thoughts that comfort and empower you in the specific situation. You can do this the minute you write down the negative thought, or you can wait till later in the day when you have more time. You can do this during your lunch break or possibly during your worry time.

Here are some examples of empowering thought replacement:

NEGATIVE : I am hurt that my teenager treats me so badly in front of his friends. Doesn't he know how much I love him and how much it hurts me?
POSITIVE : All teenagers go through this. I will not take it personally because it doesn't mean anything. He is just trying to become more independent. I will talk with him and tell him that it bothers me and that I expect to be treated with respect. If it doesn't change, I will take away some of his privileges until he changes his behavior.

NEGATIVE : She is treating me badly. What if she doesn't like me?
POSITIVE : I am overly sensitive, and it really doesn't matter if she likes me or not. I like me, and I know I am okay. I don't need

her validation. If she is treating me badly, she probably has an attitude problem, and I don't need that in my life. It is important that I make sure I am not overreacting and reading her wrong.

NEGATIVE : I feel like such a failure. I can't do anything right. I am scared.

POSITIVE : It is okay to be scared. Everybody gets scared sometimes. I am strong and capable and proud of myself. I am working toward improving myself and my life. That is a little scary, but it's also healthy and exciting.

NEGATIVE : I am worried that this health problem is something serious. What if I have some horrible disease? Maybe I shouldn't go to the doctor. What if they find something?

POSITIVE : I am just nervous because I don't know what is wrong, and that is normal. It is better for me to go to the doctor, get some answers, and know what I am dealing with so I can get beyond it. More than likely it is nothing serious, but this worrying will make me miserable. I will schedule an appointment. Then I will keep myself busy and fill myself with positive self-talk.

NEGATIVE : I hate to fly. I don't want to be on this plane. It is windy today. What if there is turbulence?

POSITIVE : It is okay that I don't love to fly. Many people get nervous flying. If there is turbulence, I know that planes fly in it all the time, and they are built to handle it. Turbulence is part of flying. It doesn't usually last long, and the pilot does his best to avoid it. I will practice my paced, diaphragmatic breathing. I will take a "goodie bag" filled with things I might need—bottled water, Mylanta, Imodium AD, Dramamine, Advil, books, tapes, snacks, etcetera. I will calm myself, talk with the person beside me, and make the most of this alone time.

Do you see what we are doing? We are defusing the power of your negative thoughts by stopping or blocking them and then replacing them with thoughts that make us feel in control. Positive replacement thoughts or statements are any thoughts or statements that make you feel happy, strong, calm, peaceful, motivated, loved, attractive, empowered, comforted, energetic, safe, and in control.

STEP 3: *Recognize that your negative thinking pattern is a bad habit, and commit yourself to breaking the habit.* It will take time, practice, and unconditional self-love because it is a difficult habit to break. As you begin to track your negative thoughts, you will become more aware of how negative you really are. You will be amazed. You will also become aware of how negative other people are. As you become more positive, you will find you have less tolerance for negative people.

STEP 4: *Begin to block your negative thoughts and to replace them with comforting, realistic, empowering thoughts.* Give yourself back the power to control how you feel and how you are affected. To make the change to a positive, productive, power thinker you must change your negative thoughts immediately, right when you have them. Stop yourself and ask, "What could I say to make myself feel better right now?" and then say it.

The more you practice, the better you will get. This technique will become an automatic response for you to take care of yourself and to empower yourself in any difficult situation, just as Diana did. You will be amazed how this one skill can change your life.

Your positive replacement thoughts don't have to be elaborate, but they do have to be believable and comforting. One helpful trick is to consider what you would say to your best friend or child if he or she were making this negative comment about himself or herself.

STEP 5: *Start taking every opportunity to be positive to others.* Look around. Whom do you love? When was the last time you told them? When was the last time you told them how wonderful they are? When was the last time you complimented your spouse or told him or her what a great lover he or she is? When was the last time you told your best friend how incredible a person he or she is and how much you appreciate him or her? When was the last time you told your mother or father what a great parent she or he has been? Have you complimented your co-workers lately? How about your boss?

Everything you do begins with a thought, thoughts create ideas, ideas create energy, and energy creates action. Positive thoughts and comments create positive energy. It feels good, it's contagious, and it's free. Spread some around, especially in your own head!

Here are some wonderful empowering statements you can begin using to make yourself feel strong and capable:

- I love life. It is stimulating and exciting. It is unpredictable, and that's okay—it keeps things interesting.
- I am a positive person who enjoys looking at things optimistically. I know nothing is easy or perfect, and I am comfortable with that.
- I like myself. I feel good about who I am and how I look. I am interesting and people enjoy my company.
- I can accomplish anything I put my mind to. I am creative and capable. Nothing can stand in my way.
- I am not afraid of taking risks; in fact, risks are exciting and productive.
- I am talented. I can accomplish whatever it is that I put my mind to.
- I am loving and compassionate. I am sensitive to others.
- I am a good problem solver. I will look for solutions and try to see the positive potential in any situation.
- I can control my anger. I will work on being an underreactor instead of an overreactor.
- I feel good. I am strong and healthy, and I have good energy.
- I am a sincere person who is comfortable with my weaknesses and my strengths.
- I am happy with my life right now, and I am looking forward to my future.
- I am calm, and I have peace of mind. I am in control of my emotions.
- I can't please everyone, and I don't want or need to. I will pick my friends carefully.
- I won't let someone else's negative energy affect me. I hold the power.

- Today is a great day, full of potential for pleasure. I am so lucky to be alive and healthy.

Feel free to use these positive thoughts as replacement thoughts for some of your negative ones, but be sure to write your own. Your own words are more believable to you, and you can make them specific to the situation, which is extremely effective.

The One Trait That Will Determine Your Life Experience

*A*ttitude is the key ingredient for living the life we desire. Our greatest tool for getting what we want is our ability to change our attitude, but attitude transformation is a skill that many of us have never learned. The truth is that our attitude will determine everything in our lives from whom we marry to what we do for a living. It will determine how we deal with our failures and how and if we achieve our successes; and it will determine our destinies. Our attitude is the defining factor that can make or break our careers, our personal relationships, our level of happiness and satisfaction. In fact, our attitudes will determine the evolution and the shape of our entire lives.

In my corporate seminars with such clients as Chrysler, AT&T, and McDonald's Corp., I asked the supervisors for the most valuable traits of their best employees. The responses I most often got are: pleasant, dedicated, positive, energetic, creative, motivated, hardworking, good with people, and responsible. I then asked, "How much money do you suppose your company has invested in offering your employees computer skills, management skills, and sales techniques?" They replied that their companies spend millions of dollars a year on this type of training, to which I responded, "When I asked you as supervisors to name the most important traits of your greatest employees, all of you named traits that would fall under the category of 'attitudes.' Did you know that the number-one reason people put out poor quality work or low effort, is poor attitude? That the number-one reason people experience job dissatisfaction is negative attitude? That the number-one reason people have co-worker problems and disputes is bad attitude?" The supervisors were intrigued.

I continued, "It has been proven that people would rather work at jobs in a positive environment and receive lots of positive feedback than work in a negative environment in which they were paid substantially more money. How much time and money has your company invested in teaching people the skill of achieving and maintaining healthy, productive attitudes?" The room often fell silent. It was a real eye-opener for those supervisors, and they agreed that a mature, healthy attitude was extremely important in any job within their company.

But attitude isn't only important to those who work or manage people. Attitude is the key ingredient to a successful, contented life. Attitude is the way you feel, your ongoing state of mind. It is how you approach something and respond to something. It is how you view life in general.

I believe that most people operate from an attitude of either negative or positive energy. In other words, you tend to see either the negative side of things or the positive. You tend to see either the glass as half empty or half full. You tend to think about the worst that could happen in a scary situation, or you think about the good that could come from it. You tend to think of all the reasons why you shouldn't do something, or you think of all the reasons why you should. Living your life with a negative attitude creates limitations and creative constipation.

I strongly suggest you take this quick attitude check to see if there any attitudes of limitation that you need to work on. In determining your attitude at the end of the test, you will find that some of the same statements may fit into different categories. Don't let that confuse you perfectionists out there!

What Does Your Attitude Say About You?

Simply answer yes or no on the following statements . . . and again, *answer honestly.*

1. I am the type of person who really needs to feel in control.

2. I am easily disappointed in myself and in others.

3. Generally speaking, I don't trust people.

4. I tend to avoid high-risk situations.

5. I like familiarity; I don't often try new things, strange food, unusual clothing styles, etc.

6. I don't like people to be angry with me or have people not like me.

7. Unexpected life changes make me uncomfortable.

8. Happy people get on my nerves.

9. I feel certain people in my life take advantage of me.

10. I am not content with my life, but I feel it would be difficult to change my situation.

11. I haven't had real fun for a long time.

12. I think the world is changing for worse.

13. I think success for many people is about luck.

14. I feel guilty easily.

15. I feel tired and unmotivated more often than I'd like to.

16. I cry easily.

17. If I want something done right I feel I have to do it myself.

18. I have problems controlling my anger.

If you answered yes to statements 1, 2, 17, and 18, you tend to be a control freak and a perfectionist. You are probably hard to please and critical, which can make it hard for you to be relaxed, satisfied, or content. You may be an angry person, and this in itself makes it hard for you to be happy or for others to be happy around you. You may be irritable and hard to please, which makes you unhappy from the starting gate. This attitude of control and perfectionism can be a very powerful tool in helping you achieve your goals, but it can also make you and everyone around you uptight. You probably need to work on learning to live with an imperfect world, and you need to work on controlling your mood swings. You need to relax and stop having such rigid standards.

If you answered yes on statements 1, 2, 3, 6, 14, and 17, you probably have unrealistic expectations about many things. This tends to go hand in hand with perfectionism. You are easily disappointed in yourself, people, situations, and the world. This makes it difficult for you to have an open mind or even to take risks because you go into things with such high expectations. You are setting yourself up for disappointment, especially from yourself. You need to lower your expectations so that you aren't always so disappointed. You need to be more relaxed, more open-minded, and less sensitive. You also have to stop trying so hard to be liked by everyone.

If you answered yes on statements 6, 9, 10, 11, and 14, you have a victim attitude. You see yourself as someone who is mistreated and treated unfairly at times. You see yourself as someone who isn't necessarily happy, but also isn't capable of changing things. You need to work on being more assertive! You give your power away. You need to take more responsibility for your own happiness and well-being. It is up to you. Stop whining and stop trying so hard not to rock the boat. It is time to rock n' roll! Get out there and take chances, be your own life jacket, say what is on your mind. Take your power back!

If you answered yes to statements 2, 3, 8, 12, and 13, you tend to be a skeptical person. This means you tend to operate from the attitude that the glass is half empty. You look at many things with a slanted eye, an eye of skepticism. You are always looking for the negative side of something. You're not what one would call open-minded or optimistic. This makes it hard because you may not recognize opportunity when it does come your way, or you may be too skeptical to even attempt to go after a dream. It also makes it hard for you to enjoy life. You need to start working on being more optimistic. This is similar to working on being a positive thinker. You must stop yourself from thinking this way and then replace negativity with the opposite positive thought about the situation.

If you answered yes to statements 4, 5, 6, 7, and 10, you are not a major risk taker. Change and risk make you uncomfortable. Your life is too predictable. This makes it hard for you to go after a dream or to change a negative situation. Come on! Life is full of challenges and anything really wonderful involves risks. Step out of your comfort zone. Do something you normally wouldn't do. Set a goal, take a chance, change your life, LIVE! You can do it. You can talk to yourself till you're blue in the face, but until you get pro-active and take action, your life won't change. What are you waiting for?

This test might provide you with some interesting personal insight, but the bottom line is this: if you have a negative attitude, it will affect your life negatively in more ways than you can imagine. It is time to recognize this trait in yourself and to begin to change it into something that works to help make your life better.

People who think with attitudes that are success oriented think like this:

The sky is the limit!
Anything is possible!

Sure I can!
Watch me!
So what if . . . ?
Don't tell me it can't be done!
It's never too late!
Try, try again!

Instead of saying, "It may be possible, but it's too difficult," try saying, "It may be difficult, but it's possible." Instead of saying "The difficult thing is . . ." try saying "The challenging thing is . . ." See the difference. Choose to look at things from a positive perspective. It really works.

A Healthy Attitude Means That You
- Are confident in yourself and your abilities.
- Feel happy and grateful most of the time.
- Enjoy life.
- See the cup as half full.
- Enjoy being around positive people.
- Stand up for yourself and have no trouble being assertive.
- Make the best of it even when things don't go your way.
- Like to try new things and enjoy taking risks.
- Have a healthy self-esteem and feel good about yourself.

The next time you're having a bad day or a bad experience, do something that our family has been doing for years: Stop and do an attitude check. Stop and ask yourself if your attitude about the situation could be the problem, and then start to re-adjust your thinking.

Attitude of Assertiveness

One of the important characteristics of a really healthy attitude is effective assertive behavior and assertive communication. You must be able to stand up for yourself and say what you feel. You must be able to express your anger in a controlled, mature, effective manner. Aggressive behavior is not assertive behavior. Many people make the mistake of believing themselves to be assertive when they are really demonstrating such aggressive behaviors as yelling, screaming, throwing fits, and losing control.

Assertive people are confident, in control of their emotions, and strong in their convictions. They are good debaters, but they are also good listeners. Assertive people are usually good problem solvers because they are good at looking at all the options and doing what makes sense. They don't always have to be right. Assertive people are open-minded and have a mature attitude.

To practice being assertive, begin by choosing to react differently in a tense or anger-producing situation. It is effective not to respond immediately but to take a ten-second to ten-minute time-out to think about your assertive response. It is important to speak with "I" messages, which indicate how you are feeling, as opposed to "you" messages, which indicate blame. For example, "When you said that the job didn't get done properly, I felt that you were implying that I didn't do my job right. What were you actually saying?" as opposed to, "You are trying to accuse me of not doing my job, and that is not true!" Do you see which one of these comments might advance to a conversation that could resolve a problem and which one might lead to a defensive response that could, in turn, lead to a heated argument that wouldn't solve anything?

You must stop yourself in a negative situation where assertive behavior would be beneficial and appropriate and ask yourself what your desired end result is. What do you want to happen as a result of your being assertive? Do you want to solve a problem? Find a solution? Communicate with someone and have him or her really listen to you and want to understand your point of view? Do you want to get something done your way?

Believe me, you will get much further with assertive behavior than you will with immature outbursts of uncontrolled anger. And you will also get a lot more respect.

When being assertive, always maintain good eye contact, speak in a controlled tone of voice, and think before you respond. Keep your sentences short, use "I" messages, and focus on what you want to happen, what you want as an end result. You will be amazed at how effective assertive behavior is. If you have ever been in the company of someone who has mastered the skill of assertive behavior, you have seen the power in this skill. It is difficult not to be impressed by or at times even intimidated by someone who is assertive, confident, in control, and determined.

Recently I saw a wonderful example of assertive behavior demonstrated beautifully by a frustrated father. My family was on vacation. We had booked an excursion through the hotel's concierge, and I was down in the reservations room picking up our tickets when I was privy to the following scenario.

A man in his late thirties came in with three young children. They were all excited and carrying snorkel gear. He proceeded to ask a woman behind the counter what time the snorkel sail was leaving and stated that he had come to pick up his tickets. The agent looked through the day's schedule and looked up in slight embarrassment. "I'm sorry sir. That snorkel trip has been canceled for today because that boat was booked for a large, private party. They should have informed you, but sometimes they miss someone. I am so sorry. I can refund your money." The man looked puzzled. "But I booked this snorkel sail two months ago through your service. I have the reservation numbers right here." He gave them to her and then he continued. "We have people joining us on this trip who have driven over an hour just to get here. We bought their tickets in advance, too." He was not angry just direct. "I'm sorry, sir, there is nothing I can do. There are no other boats available. We will refund your money," the woman repeated again with very little sincerity in her voice. As she talked to him, she continued with busy work at the counter and continued to answer the phone. He then decided to get assertive. "Excuse me, Miss, I would appreciate your full attention right now. I would appreciate it if you would not answer the phone or work on something else until we resolve this matter so we can all get on with our day." I watched in amazement as she put down the phone and her busy work and looked him in the eye, albeit she was frustrated! He went on with a very assertive voice tone and very direct eye contact. In fact it would have been difficult for her *not* to return his gaze. "I have seven people who have planned their day around this snorkeling trip. Simply refunding our money doesn't solve the problem. This is an error that someone else made. We need an activity for the day that is acceptable to us. If you can't authorize this, I am happy to talk with your supervisor." It was clear this man was strong and determined. She knew he was right, and she knew he wasn't going away until it was resolved to his satisfaction. His body language, eye contact, and tone of voice made that very clear. It was amazing to see what happened next. Within minutes the woman was on the phone. She lined up a *private* excursion on a smaller boat, just for their party, and she gave them dinner coupons for seven in the main dinning room. I am certain the value of that packet far exceeded his originally scheduled package. He thanked her, gathered his things, and left, satisfied.

Had he not been assertive, he would have left frustrated and disappointed, with nothing to do for the day. He would have gotten a refund, but that wasn't what he wanted. He wanted an activity for his family and friends on this one day of vacation that they had planned together. He got that and a wonderful dinner to top the day off with! What a great example of how effective assertive behavior can be when done correctly. I only wish I would have had that one on video!

Reclaim Your Power

It is time to reclaim your power. You must learn to appreciate yourself, right now, exactly as you are, even though there are things you would like to change. You must begin to believe in yourself and know that you are incredible and full of potential. It all begins with attitude and what you say when you talk to yourself. Don't give your power away. Don't let a negative attitude or negative thinking, yours or someone else's, keep you from living a fun, full, contented life. Begin now to change the person you are to the person you know you have the potential to become.

9

HOW TO TURN A DIFFICULT

PAST INTO A

DYNAMIC FUTURE

Life is a series of experiences, each one of which makes us bigger, even though sometimes it's hard to realize this; for the world was built to develop character, and we must learn that the setbacks and grief which we endure help in our marching onward.

— HENRY FORD

This excerpt was taken from *Interview* magazine in April 2000:

"I don't think I was the happiest kid. So maybe performing gave me that outlet for a certain sort of attention that I wasn't getting. I felt lonely. We lived in a trailer park, and the kids who went to my school seemed to be more upper class. When I was in about eighth grade I remember, and this is something I

haven't talked about, something that happened. A group of kids who I thought were my friends ran past me and threw this letter at me. It hit me in the head, and I was like, 'What the heck?' I took the letter, and they ran off giggling. I think I got on the school bus, and I opened up that letter, and it said, 'You think you're so cool, but you're not; you think you're so pretty, but you're ugly; you think you're so talented, but you suck.' I was heartbroken. I still can't figure it out. I don't think I did anything to deserve it.

"When I was sixteen, my mom was at a crossroads in her life, and I knew I wanted to be an actor. We picked up, with seventy-five bucks to our name, and drove down to California in our old Oldsmobile Cutlass Supreme. We lived off our Mobil card—you know, you can go into the mini-marts in Mobil stations and eat."

This powerful, intimate excerpt was taken from an interview with the young, up-and-coming actress and Oscar winner, Hillary Swank, who won the award for best actress this year for her performance in *Boys Don't Cry*. Among her competitors were Meryl Streep and Annette Benning. What do think her old school chums are saying now? Success is the best revenge.

The youngest child of an accountant and a chronically ill mother, he was in ninth grade when his father lost his job, plunging the family into poverty. The family of six wound up living out of a Volkswagen van. Some of the kids quit school and worked maintenance jobs at a local tire rim factory. His bedridden mother, whom he often attempted to cheer up with his funny anecdotes, died of kidney failure before she ever had the chance to see how successful her talented son would become.

He has seen phenomenal success as a comic genius in such movies as *Ace Ventura Pet Detective*, *Dumb and Dumber*, and *The Mask*. The past few years have proven that inside that rubbery body lurked not just a fabulous comedian, but also a genuinely sensitive and talented actor, as Jim Carrey went on to star in *The Truman Show* and *Man on the Moon*.

Stoic. Such is the prevailing image of seventy-year-old Ethel Kennedy, who in the past half-century has raised eleven children and survived losses of the most monumental kind: her parents and a brother killed in separate plane crashes, her husband and his brother murdered, and two sons dead. Who says the rich have it easier?

How has she survived such tragedy and still managed to hold herself and her life together? Those who know her well say it is a matter of faith. She goes to mass every day and prays before every meal and before she goes to bed at night. She doesn't dwell on the negative. She swims several times a week and immerses herself in a whirlwind of charity work. She is the founder and the guiding light for the Robert F. Kennedy Memorial, which funds humanitarian projects around the world.

"She's the greatest source of strength to all of us," says her daughter Kathleen Kennedy Townsend, Maryland's lieutenant governor. "She's filled with love. She makes people feel special. She has a terrific sense of humor. She is a doer."

As a result of a terrible automobile accident, a young woman named Nancy Martenario was left handicapped and in a wheelchair. Her life crumbled. First she lost her job. Then her husband left her. Life is not fair. She was left to deal with depression and frustration. She constantly found herself cursing her ugly, non–user-friendly method of transportation, the wheelchair.

Mustering up all her energy and funneling all of her creative juices into a positive direction toward something about which she was passionate, she designed prettier and more user-friendly wheelchairs.

Nancy is now a highly successful businesswoman and entrepreneur. She owns a company that manufactures the number-one-selling wheelchair in the world. It is colorful and easy to use and has helped to change the stigma attached to wheelchairs— and the people who use them—forever.

She was not your average, fair-skinned, Midwestern five-year-old. She was slightly chubby, her lips were too big for her face, she was "different" looking; and not in a way that went over well in a small town in Ohio. Something about her was ethnic. Her hair was dark and so were her eyes, and her skin was a warm brown. Was she Indian, Italian, or Hispanic maybe? She didn't have the luxury of knowing, for her father was adopted and didn't have a clue as to his nationality or family history. The one thing they could be certain of was that alcoholism lurked somewhere in his gene pool.

She remembers lying in that pale green bedroom just off the kitchen on many fear-filled nights, waiting for "him" to come home. He would stumble in, cursing to himself, rattling the pots and pans while attempting to fix something to eat. Sometimes he'd manage to make something to eat, sometimes he'd just pass out, and sometimes he'd get mean. What would he do this time? Should she be afraid? Should she hide the knives just in case? Fear of knives was just one of her many obsessions.

Life wasn't easy, back then. Holidays were always challenging because they gave her father a reason to drink. He never had money for birthday presents or Christmas because he drank it all away. Friendships were difficult to maintain because everyone knew her father was an alcoholic . . . everyone except for him. And she never knew what she would find when she brought someone home. Would her dad be passed out, or would he be obnoxious and belittle her in front of her friends?

She lived in an old house beside a railroad track at the end of a dead-end street. Her dad bought it for $7,000 in 1962 as a peace offering to her mother, with the promise of a new life. Things would be better; he would be better. This girl loved her dad in spite of himself. They all did. When he was sober, life was good. He had class—you know, the inborn kind. When he was sober, he would buy her mom the finest chocolates on Valentine's Day and take the family out to dinner to fine restaurants that he couldn't afford.

She remembers walking with him, so proud, holding his hand as he whistled. He always whistled when he was happy. She can still smell the scent of the match as he went to light his cigarette. Memories. She remembers the refrigerator being pushed to the floor and running out into the snow in her bare feet to the neighbors' house because "daddy was mad." She remembers lying in her bed in the green bedroom shaking with fear. Did he really have a gun? Would daddy hurt mommy? Would daddy hurt her? She remembers the police dragging her daddy down the sidewalk as she ran after him screaming for them to leave him alone.

She found comfort in her mother's arms, but many times in spite of her young age, she was the one doing the comforting. Her mother was very strong and yet sensitive. Her mother loved her father very much. But how many nights did her mother cry? How many times did her brothers attempt to protect them all and bring their dad to his senses, one more time? Her family's entire life revolved around her father and his drinking.

As she grew up, she wondered about her own life. Everything seemed like such a struggle and people from "her type" of family didn't really go anywhere . . . did they? Was the dead-end street any indication of what was to be her future? She remembers lying in bed hearing that train whistle blowing, wishing she could just hop on and run away, to a better life, to a safer place.

As she matured, she knew she wasn't worthy. She envied her friends with their fine families and perfect lives. She dreamed of a better life for her family. She dreamed of a better life for herself. She fantasized about becoming "somebody" and dreamed of doing something "big" someday, something that mattered. One thing was for sure, she knew she could comfort people and make people feel better. That was her role in the family, after all, her training ground. Little did she know that her ability to comfort people would play a major role in her life as an adult. Her dream to be somebody and to do something that mattered came true. That little girl was me.

I understand pain, embarrassment, and fear. I understand feelings of inadequacy and humiliation. I know the feeling of abandonment and that constant edgy feeling that something bad is about to happen. I understand what people are feeling when they say they think good things don't last and that something will surely ruin it all. I know what it's like to be talked about, made fun of, and tortured by your peers. I know what pain and low self-esteem is all about. I can't leave my seminars until the last needy person feels validated. I can't walk away from someone who is devastated. I can't not reach out when someone is in pain. I can't help sticking up for someone of whom others are making fun. I can't help fighting for the underdog. I can't stop myself from trying to make others feel better in their darkest hour. I am determined to show them the light at the end of the tunnel—the way, if there is a will, and the will if there isn't any. I am driven to give people hope.

When I was a young adult, I blamed all my problems and insecurities on my father's alcoholism and the life that resulted from it. And there's no doubt it was responsible for a great deal of my problems and insecurities. But his weakness is also responsible for who I am today. His behavior created character and compassion in a way nothing else could have. It certainly paved the way for my "mission" and the life I live now. When one of my children met a friend with an alcoholic parent, I taught him to be understanding and not to get caught up in the gossip and ridicule. When I meet clients who grew up with abuse or abandonment issues, I show them how to use that pain to motivate them toward a better life. When I find someone struggling with a family member who demands all the attention, whether it's from alcoholism, illness, or emotional instability, I can offer support and make suggestions for coping. When people tell me they have no self-esteem and no confidence because of what they went through as a child, I know how to get them to start dreaming again and what to tell them to do to get their identity back. I know all of this because I've been there. My life experience was a necessary part in the journey that led me to help others who struggle. It's that simple, and yet somehow, it's equally profound.

Eventually my mother divorced my father, in spite of how much she and we all loved him. It was a difficult thing for her to do, but she did it to stop the chaos. Looking back, I wouldn't trade my past and my childhood for anything. I had and still have a wonderful mother who taught me the meaning of unconditional love, simplicity, and patience. She taught me what it means to be a good mother and a dedicated life partner.

I had a great father, too, but he had a terrible illness. I understood why she loved him so much and why she tried time and time again to help him heal and to make it work. He was quite special, and I was fortunate to inherit some of his good traits: his ability to be entertaining and social, his sense of style, his musical ability, his sense of humor, and his drive to do big things in life. The only regret I have is that he didn't become sober and live to give my mother the type of lifelong partnership she yearned for with him, and only him. She deserved that and so much more. But that is something I had no control over—no one did, it appears—not even him.

Living in the Past Isn't Living

Many of us could claim a difficult past. Possibly you grew up with an alcoholic parent. Maybe you were abused in some way. Some of us might use the excuse of being adopted. Others might claim neglect by parents or a parent who was never available. Maybe you didn't have parents. Maybe you didn't have a childhood. I know many people who feel their lack of happiness, success, or contentment as an adult is a direct result of their unhealthy childhood. These people are still dwelling on, if not living in, their past.

Others of us have had difficulties as adults that could justify our unhappy present moment. If we have been through a difficult situation, it could make us fearful or gun-shy, so to speak; it could make us poor risk takers and even victims. If we have struggled in some horrible way through a tough, painful experience, it could make us feel vulnerable and weak. On the other hand, it could make us grateful, impassioned, and more willing to take risks.

It can be healthy to review the past and to try to heal from it. But it is unhealthy and unproductive to get stuck there. Who couldn't blame their parents for something? Who of us couldn't trace some of our negative characteristics back to a relative or a past experience? What adult hasn't struggled and been in pain in his other life? Who of us hasn't experienced rejection, loss, and feelings of insecurity?

The difference, though, in who is successful and who isn't, isn't based on what we have or haven't been through. It is based on what we choose to do with our experiences. This is what makes all the difference in the world, or certainly in a life.

As I've mentioned before, I believe people tend to be either optimistic or pessimistic. One gives you power, the other takes it away. When you feel as if you don't have any power, you start looking for excuses for why not. "It's because I was the middle child." "It is because my father was never around." "It's because my mother was an alcoholic." "It's because I was abused." "It is because I've been rejected." "I have had so many losses in my life that I can't deal with anymore."

Using Your Past as Motivation

Can you see how you might take these same experiences and use them to create opportunities?

"It was because I was the middle child that I have learned to become a great negotiator and to be independent." "Because my father was never around, I now realize the importance of being there for my kids, and I have decided to make better parenting choices as a father for my children." "Because my mother was an alcoholic, I am sensitive to other people who struggle with this disease and will learn to handle my issues in a healthy way." "Because I was abused, I am sensitive to others who have been hurt in anyway." "I will not let rejection scare me because I have survived it so many times before." "I have had so many losses in my life that it makes me grateful to be alive at all, and more open to taking risks because of the realization that life is short and a precious gift."

Do you think it's possible that Hillary Swank was driven to

become a successful actor partially because of an underlying need to prove something to herself and others? Do you think Jim Carrey's difficult childhood of poverty and struggle encouraged much of his humor and his ambition? Do you think there is any doubt that Ethel Kennedy appreciates life and lives with tremendous gratitude because the adversity that she's experienced has made her intensely aware of how precious life is? And how about Nancy Martenario? Isn't it obvious that her terrible car accident, although tragic, is what led her to make a powerful positive difference in the world and in her own life? You might wonder if any of these people, including myself, would be who they are or where they are now if they hadn't experienced such adversity in their lives.

Life is wonderful, but it is challenging. The only thing you can be certain of is that most things in life aren't certain. Change and challenge are certain though. And when they come our way, we can run and hide, or we can open our minds to the next phase of life they bring with them and plunge forward with an attitude of optimism and confidence in our ability to handle it, whatever "it" may be. "It" could lead to a whole new way of living, a whole new journey or calling. Sometimes the most difficult situations we can imagine create the most incredible opportunities.

But it is hard when you are in the struggle to recognize this. I believe we are all here for a reason. I believe we struggle with certain challenges in life so that we can help others deal with similar issues. I really believe we all have a mission. But it is up to us to find that mission and to hear the calling. Possibly your mission is to be a great parent, or maybe your mission is in just being someone who gives positive energy and reinforcement to others by virtue of being who you are. We aren't all supposed to save the world; some of us have a hard enough time just saving ourselves. But when we do manage to overcome some difficulty, I think it is our universal duty to help someone else save themselves if we can and if the opportunity arises.

Many years ago when I was severely agoraphobic. Life was torturous for me. I was so overwhelmed with fear and anxiety that I couldn't function normally. I was afraid to fly (what if the plane crashed or I went crazy on the plane?), afraid to drive more than a few miles from home (what if I freaked out and wrecked the car?). I hated going shopping, and I didn't like to socialize (what if I panicked and made a fool of myself, what would people think?). And forget going anywhere where there wasn't a restroom close by (what if I had an attack of irritable bowel syndrome?).

My life was a living hell and becoming more and more limited. I remember being afraid to even talk on the phone because I might say the wrong thing. I was so miserable and overwhelmed with my thoughts. I remember wondering if my past had caused this weird anxiety and fear. Could it be a result of my father's alcoholism? Could it be a result of his violent temper and rages? Could it be an aftermath of my feeling insecure and unworthy as a child and an adolescent?

I remember one night when I was particularly struggling. I was alone in my apartment wondering how I was going to make it through another day. I was curled up in a ball on my sofa in the living room, crying. I was afraid, I was depressed, and I felt so alone and hopeless. I just wanted to turn my mind off and stop the racing, ruminating fearful thoughts, but I didn't know how to do it. I remember thinking that night that I couldn't go on. I couldn't live like that any longer. But I was afraid of dying—and I was afraid of living. There was no answer.

Little did I know way back then that all this suffering was going to force me to face my lifelong fears head on. And little did I know, in the midst of all that pain, that my suffering would lead to a life of helping others overcome their fears. I never would have begun to even think it possible that such a horrible thing could turn around and become something so beautiful, if not one of the greatest blessings in my life.

Of course, it didn't happen overnight, and it wasn't in any way easy. It was a gradual unveiling, a gentle climb up a very steep mountain, with one step forward and two steps back. But it was a path I had to take and I knew it, a calling I had to heed. It was and is a beautiful example of turning tragedy into triumph. If I can do it, so can you. I am no different or better than you. I just followed my heart and let myself step out of my comfort zone. I stopped blaming my past, my father, my childhood, and anyone or anything else I could blame. I stopped saying "Life's not fair," and I started to grow up and take responsibility for my own happiness.

Turning Negative into Positive

Take a few moments to think of negative situations that you have experienced, the ones that still haunt you in some way, and begin to think of ways you could bring something positive out of them.

Let's take a look at some of the ways you can begin to turn negative experiences and challenges from your past into positive energy and motivation to help yourself create a better life now and in the future:

Acknowledge the experience: Acknowledge the difficulties in your past that you believe are still affecting you now in some way. Think them through, and write a brief paragraph about how these experiences have affected you both negatively and positively.

Let go of it emotionally: What steps could you begin to take to eliminate the guilt, anger, or fear associated with these issues? Could you talk with a person who was involved and gain a new, healthier perspective? Could you apologize or ask for an apology? Could you write a letter or forgive someone? How can you let go of the negative emotion associated with this experience?

Plan your course of action: What steps can you begin to take today and tomorrow to overcome your fear and insecurities? Do you need to take a course or to get therapy? Do you need to set yourself up to face your fear head on?

Find a grief partner: Find someone who understands your pain and the pain associated with this type of problem, someone you can talk to. It would be great to find someone, even a support group, who has been through a similar experience and handled it in a positive way. It is time to share the secret, tell the story, and let go of the pain.

Find your mission: Describe one or two ways that you could use this past experience to benefit others in some way. It will help in the letting go, and it will help in the healing process. Could you volunteer or help a friend to heal?

Practice pro-active reflection: Only allow yourself to think about this specific issue from now on as a method of pro-active reflection. Describe how you are going to use this experience to move yourself toward some positive action. How can it motivate you to take risks and to make changes in your life for the good?

Write a paragraph describing all the positive things about the type of person you are now, as a result of where you've come from and what you have been through. Be sure to be loving, positive, and descriptive. Refer to this paragraph whenever you feel the urge to start reminiscing in any negative way or feeling sorry for yourself.

The past is over, it doesn't exist anymore; and because you can't go back and change it, the only thing you can do is use it for motivation to help you make better choices about the present and the future. Thinking back on the tough times can be a tremendous source of motivation.

Several years ago a college professor of psychology and sociology, said to me, "Lucinda, you seem to have so much drive and ambition. Where do you think it comes from?" After giving it some thought, I realized that much of my drive has come from memories: memories of my mother's old rusty car fenders; memories of pushing our groceries home in a cart during the times when we had no car; memories of being ashamed of these things; memories of living with an angry, alcoholic parent; memories of my sister dying of cancer; memories of being stifled and horrified by severe panic attacks. These are some of my motivations. These were all difficult times, but they motivated me to work hard, to stay grateful and humble, to not take anything for granted, to not complain, and to live in the moment. These experiences have motivated me to take tremendous risks and to go after my dreams because life is such a precious gift.

If it weren't for these past experiences, I wouldn't be who I am now, nor would I be doing all the wonderful things I am doing. That is the power of using your negative past experiences positively.

Turning a Difficult Past into a Desirable Future

Going after our dreams in relationship to overcoming past-related issues and challenges involves three important characteristics:

1. Persistence.

2. The ability to take risks comfortably.

3. The capacity to forgive.

Let's look more closely at the importance of these character-istics and their relationship to dealing with issues or misconceptions about ourselves that are related to our past.

Persistence

Just recently I read a story about Wilma Rudolph. She was one of twenty-two children. When she was young, she contracted double pneumonia and scarlet fever that left her paralyzed in one leg. Doctors said she probably would never walk again. At the age of nine she took the brace off her leg and began to walk. In her early teens, she decided to start running. She was horrible at first. Every race she entered over the next several years found her coming in last. Everyone around her told her she should just quit, but she continued.

Even though she was exhausted and discouraged, she kept running. Finally, her efforts paid off and she won her first race. That was the beginning of a career in running that became her life's passion. She continued to work hard, to train hard, and to win various races around the world. As time passed and her skill improved, she went for the gold, literally. This incredible young woman, who was told at one time that she might never walk again, went on to win three Olympic gold metals.

This is an extreme and wonderful example of the power of persistence. But for many people just sticking to one thing long enough to see the fruits of their efforts is difficult. If they are filling themselves with negative messages about themselves due to past experiences, it makes persistence twice as challenging. It is hard to keep trying if you typically fail; it is hard to keep plug-ging away if you secretly see yourself as lazy or incapable; it is difficult if not impossible to stay motivated when things look bleak if you see yourself as someone who gives up easily.

Sometimes I feel as if we are all running. Only we're not winning gold metals. We're running from ourselves and from our past, we're running from our fears. But self-esteem and happiness can only be achieved when we come to terms with our past, get comfortable with who we are, and feel that we are worthy. It is hard to feel capable and confident when your past keeps getting in the way. Once you deal with your past and learn to use it as motivation rather than as an excuse, you will be amazed at what you are capable of.

When you are persistent, you simply don't give up. You stay focused on your goal and stay determined no matter what others say, no matter how challenging, because you know what you want and why you want it. It may take years, and it probably will, but you know it's worth it. And besides, you are enjoying the pursuit, remember?

You don't let past failures or self-misconceptions get in the way. Maybe you weren't a stick-to-it type of person before, but you are now. Maybe you have failed in the past, but it doesn't mean you will fail again. You stay determined.

In my opinion—and I have seen this in working with successful people—persistence is one of the most important attributes a person can have. It is often the determining factor in whether someone attains a goal or realizes a dream.

Taking Calculated Risks

When it comes to being a great risk taker, it helps tremendously to follow a plan of action that will guarantee success on some level. You wouldn't go out and audition for a part in a major film without some training. You wouldn't purchase property without doing an inspection. You wouldn't invest in a project without doing some research. You wouldn't get up in front of business people and give a presentation without doing some preparation. Anything that leads to a positive end result takes preparation. So does risk taking. People who are afraid to take risks are afraid because they don't know how to do it, or because they've done it in the past and failed, or because they don't have enough information, or because they are uncomfortable with making decisions.

I've found that many people are afraid to take risks because they doubt their ability to make good decisions. Some people suffer from what I refer to as *decision-making phobia*.

Do you:

- Fear making a mistake? "What if I make the wrong decision, what if I can't turn back?"
- Lack confidence in your own judgment?
- Change your mind often? Waffle back and forth—first you want this, then you want that, then you're not even sure anymore?
- Have a hard time with commitment?

These are sure signs of being a bad decision maker, which will result in an inability to take risks comfortably. If you are having a hard time making a decision, look for an underlying cause. It is usually fear. What are you afraid of that is specifically related to this decision? Once you've determined what your fear is, ask yourself if what you want is worth the risk. What do you have to win if you move forward and take that leap of faith? Is the reward worth it, in spite of your fears?

Guidelines for Risk Taking

If what you want is worth taking a risk, here are some guidelines that will help you to take risks with confidence and comfort:

1. *Start with a clean slate. This is a new time in your life, and you are a different person. Don't let old memories do anything but motivate you.* A man I worked with a few years ago had had a very difficult life. He was a recovering alcoholic; he had a history of bad relationships; and he had a hard time sticking to one job for very long. Here he was in his late forties reevaluating things and wanting to get his life together. He had a dream of opening a surfing shop. He surfed all of his life, and surfing was one thing he really knew about. He found a small storefront, talked to the right people, got some financing, and made his dream come true. The first year was tough though, and he recalls falling into the old familiar negative messages about himself. But he stood firm. The second year, word of mouth spread, and he started to draw a following. People liked his style and his stories. His store was homey and "beachy," unlike many of the big sport stores in the area. His business thrived. Finally, he had contentment, security, and an identity of which he was proud.

2. *Identify your needs and desires relative to the decision, or the risk, and rank them in the level of importance.* For example, when we made the decision to move to California, we wrote down

exactly what our needs and desires were and the order in which they were important to us. We wanted to live by the water, but we decided it was more important initially to live in a neighborhood for the kids' sake, so we moved into a neighborhood. We wanted to buy a house, but more important we wanted to take time to decide if we liked California and to look around to decide what area we would want to live in. So we rented for the first year. These were choices we made based on level of importance.

3. *Gather all the information you can in regard to the alternatives, what you will need to do as far as a plan of action, what steps you need to take, and the advantages and disadvantages.* Recently a woman came to me who wanted to start her own business. I suggested she write up a plan of action detailing the things she needed to do and the people she needed to talk to. I even gave her the name of someone who had started a similar business and suggested she meet with her for insight. She found this extremely helpful and felt that it saved her much unnecessary research work up front.

4. *Make a decision, choose the direction in which you're going to go, and be committed to making that one work.* Remember there is no wrong decision. You choose the most appropriate one based on your intuition and the information you have gathered. Recently a friend of mine had a difficult but wonderful opportunity. He was offered two incredible job opportunities at the same time. The anxiety of not being able to make a decision nearly destroyed him. He was so afraid he would choose the wrong job. I suggested he follow his gut: choose

one and then commit himself to making it work. Once he did, he soared, and he was greatly relieved from the stress of the indecision.

5. *Begin forming a plan of action to get to your goal, and choose the most realistic path. Choose a path that has the greatest and most realistic opportunity for success.* The most realistic path may not be the fastest. Remember the woman who wanted to be a painter but chose a path that would allow her to live the lifestyle she wanted and raise a family? Look at all the different options. There are many. How many different ways could you get to your goal, and which would work best for you?

6. *Shoot for the stars. Give it all your time, your energy, your positive anticipation. Give it all your determination and dedication.* If you are going into anything half motivated, don't expect it to work. I just recently worked with a woman who moved to Los Angeles to be an actor. She had been there for two years and was frustrated and disappointed that she hadn't really achieved her goal of "making it" within two years. She thought she might as well go home. She has the wrong attitude. She needs to make a decision that acting is something she wants to do more than anything and that she is passionate about it and willing to give it her all, no matter how long it takes. Two years is nothing to achieve a dream of that magnitude. If you are passionate and determined maybe you are don't want it that badly.

7. *Be flexible. Your desires may change along the way or open a different door. And that's okay, if it's okay with you.* Trust yourself

and the universe. Allow yourself the comfort of knowing that nothing is set in stone. You can almost always change your mind.

8. Finally, *just do it, because if you don't try, you'll never know and that in itself will give you anxiety.* You start winning when you stop whining, and you stop procrastinating and you start beginning. It is that simple.

Ask yourself the following questions, and write the answers in your journal:

What do you want right now that would take some risk?

How would you feel if you got what you want?

How would this change your life?

How strong is your belief right now that you can make this happen?

During the next three days, what risks could you take that would move you one step closer to this goal?

Forgiveness

Holding on to anger is like grasping a hot coal with the intent of throwing it at someone else; you are the one who gets burned.

—BUDDHA

I remember a man named Allen who was in one of our group sessions. He was harboring a tremendous amount of anger toward his family. All his life he felt as though his father favored his brother. When Allen and his brother were growing up, his father and brother went on sailing trips together. Allen didn't like to sail because he got seasick. His brother and father both enjoyed going to baseball games, another activity Allen neither enjoyed nor participated in. Allen's brother eventually went to work with his father in the family business. Allen didn't really want to work in the family business, partly because he felt like such an outsider when it came to his father and brother. But the hurtful part was that he wasn't invited. The father and brother just assumed it didn't interest him.

As time passed, the brother took over the business, worked hard, and did very well. He was eventually given the entire company in stocks and inheritance. Allen built his own successful company without any help or financial assistance from his parents. He didn't ask, and they didn't offer. He went on to marry and have children. He was great husband, a wonderful father, and a successful businessman.

Still, Allen was resentful and hurt about his relationship with his father and his brother, and it was affecting his life greatly. He felt that he was always second in line for his father's attention and that his brother was favored by both of his parents. Allen felt that his brother was given an incredible opportunity by getting the family business and that he was given nothing. I have to admit, after hearing the different experiences he had been through with his family, it did appear that way. His pain and resentment were justifiable, but were they healthful and productive? After discussing this issue with the group for several weeks, Allen decided to talk with his father about his feelings. He got nowhere. His dad kept the conversation very superficial and never really addressed the real issue, Allen's feelings of neglect and favoritism toward his brother.

It was very obvious that nothing was going to change and that his parents weren't ever going to see it as Allen did. He was never going to get his father to be the kind of father he had longed for his whole life. Allen was never going to get the validation he wanted from any of them. What should he do? His first inclination was to disown them all and never see them again. But this was his family, and his children's only grandparents, since his wife's parents were deceased.

After considering his various options, we talked about what he could gain by lowering his expectations and forgiving them. At first he was outraged. He couldn't even conceive of that option. As we talked, he began to see that he was the only one suffering. They were insensitive to his pain and would continue to be. They certainly weren't in any pain. By holding on to his anger and resentment, he would continue to feel bitter, and they would continue to have a negative effect on him, without even trying. They wouldn't be affected, just he would be. At least by letting go of the anger and understanding that they were incapable of giving him what he wanted and accepting that that was who they were, he could begin to heal. He could maintain a relationship with them that would still offer family connections for his children.

He had a great life; he had nothing to be envious of. By letting go of the anger and forgiving his family, he would feel better and more at peace. He could accept the relationship for what it was, get what he could from it, and not take the rest of it personally. By forgiving them, he was letting go of the negative emotion of anger and pain. By holding on to the anger, he would gain nothing and be miserable. He would suffer, and so would his children. He forgave them, expected less from them, and let go of the anger. He feels so much more peaceful, and he sincerely believes his release of the negative emotions has allowed wonderful new experiences to come into his life.

Often people think that the only way they can forgive someone is if that person apologizes and feels genuinely remorseful. It is wonderful to ask for an apology and even more wonderful to get one, but life usually isn't that simple. The real healing comes when you are able to forgive regardless of what the other person does or does not do. When you are able to forgive in your mind and in your heart, you allow yourself to let go of the negative emotion so you aren't hurt by it anymore. When you master the skill of *forgiveness,* you understand that it is about letting go and moving on, without attitude and without anger. Forgiveness is about acceptance of reality and a clear, mature understanding that you can't control other people. It is about lowering your expectations and coming to terms with what is and what will be. And then it comes back around to you—it always does. If you aren't happy, successful, or content, it's not someone else's fault anymore. Use that pain as motivation, and use that feeling of neglect to help build better relationships with people you know will respond to you. Prove something to yourself . . . prove that you are capable, lovable, secure within yourself, and able to look at things maturely. Prove that your expectations are realistic and that you are capable of letting go of worthless negative emotion. Prove to yourself that no one and nothing is perfect and that different people will fill different needs in your life, and that's okay.

Forgiveness isn't about "them" (the person or people with whom you are angry), it isn't about whether they are worthy of being forgiven or whether they want to be forgiven, or whether they even know they've been forgiven. Forgiveness begins and ends with you. It empowers you because you simply let go of the issue and choose to be less affected. It also offers you peace of mind. You let it go, turn it over to God, and move on.

I believe that when you forgive and let go of the negative energy associated with that issue or person for whom you were harboring anger, you open a door that allows positive, healthy new energy to come your way.

The Present of Today Is the Past of Tomorrow

Use your past as motivation for success and empowerment instead of as an excuse for weakness and procrastination. Let your past work for you in some positive way. Let go of the bitterness, anger, and resentment. Don't let it hold you back or keep you from being happy. This day, this moment, and the future are yours to do with what you will. Right now you are creating what will eventually become the past for yourself and others . . . make good memories.

10

INTUITION AND

DIVINE SIGNS

By learning to contact, listen to, and act on our intuition, we can directly connect to the higher power of the universe and allow it to become our guiding force.

— SHAKTI GAWAIN

Mom and I always had great "long distance" talks on Saturday mornings, but on this particular weekend, something was different. She sounded a bit confused and disoriented over the phone. "Are you feeling all right, Mom?" I asked her.

"Oh, I'm all right," she said. "I think I might have the flu or something. I'm going to the doctor on Monday. But don't worry; I'm sure it's nothing." Then we continued our mother-daughter Saturday-morning-ritual phone conversation.

I called her again on Sunday, and she still sounded a little strange. Again, she reassured me that it was just the flu. I would have run right over there, but because I had moved to Los Angeles several years earlier, and she still lived in Ohio, that wasn't possible.

On Monday morning, I called to find her still confused and

somewhat forgetful. "Mom," I said, "what time is your doctor's appointment?"

"Oh, yes. I nearly forgot. I should leave soon."

"Call me the minute you get home."

"I will," she said.

I left for a meeting a few minutes later, but as I was driving down the street, I had an overwhelming feeling that something was really wrong with my mother. My intuition kept telling me to turn around and take immediate action, so I did. I hurried back into the house and called the doctor's office. "I want my mother admitted to the hospital immediately," I said to the nurse in a firm voice. "I know my mother, and I just know something is wrong with her. I'm catching a plane home tonight."

The woman at the other end of the line was not very supportive, and neither was the doctor. "We think you're overreacting, Mrs. Bassett," she said. "But we'll honor your request."

I hung up, phoned the airlines, and then I canceled my appointments for the next few days. By early evening, I was at the airport. Just before I boarded the plane, I called my mother at the hospital. "I'm cold and I'm scared," she said, and she started to cry. *Thank God, she's in the hospital*, I thought. "I'm on my way, Mom," I said, trying to reassure her. "Just hang in there, and I'll be there as soon as I can. I love you."

That evening, my mother experienced a stroke and a related seizure. Had she not been admitted into the hospital that afternoon, she probably would have died during the night, in her home, all alone. I shudder to think that if I hadn't followed my intuition, my mother probably would not be alive today.

Life is filled with choices, some more difficult than others. Should I stay or should I go? Should I do the deal or walk away?

Should I take the chance or play it safe? Should I follow my heart or go with my gut?

We Must Trust Our Instincts

A goose flies by a chart which the Royal Geographical Society could not improve.

—HOLMES

Gut feelings and instincts are part of a powerful resource called intuition. You may think that paying attention to your "gut feelings" sounds a bit silly. Perhaps you think that divine guidance is a far-fetched idea or that synchronistic events in your life are completely coincidental. It's okay if you feel this way. I only ask you to keep an open mind because the more we learn to trust these concepts, the more confident we will become in trusting our intuition and the more likely we are to stay on the right path and to get what we really want. On the other hand, the less we trust our inner feelings, the more likely we are to turn to others for advice. Then, all too often, we base our decisions solely on outside information. We simply don't trust ourselves.

I'm not suggesting there's anything wrong with gathering different perspectives from people whom you admire and respect. But if you don't ultimately follow your own instincts and intuition, your own inside information, you might find yourself walking down the wrong path. It is easy to get confused, to place importance on the wrong information, and to end up frustrated and deprived of the happiness you deserve and desire.

Intuition gives you a bigger picture. It takes into account your personal life and the world around you. It is about being true to yourself and to what is right universally. Unfortunately, the times we live in are so bombarded with practical applications and information that paying attention to our intuition seems almost absurd. However, I ask you to consider this: Can you think of times in your life when following your gut might have changed your path? Can you remember a situation where going with your initial instinct about something would have changed the outcome, possibly bringing you closer to the life for which you are still striving? If you answered yes, ask yourself why you ignored those signs. Did you not trust yourself? Did you go in a different direction because of fear or outside influences or lack of faith in your own insight? How much more time are you willing to waste, how many more opportunities are you willing to ignore, because you don't know yourself well enough to trust your own messages? Intuition is such an important resource and such a big part of creating a life of success, health, abundance, and happiness.

Take a moment, and on a separate piece of paper or in your journal, fill in the following blanks. Don't overanalyze the sentences or your responses. Just write a word or a thought, whatever immediately comes to mind.

Someday when I am _____, I am going to finally _____.

This will make me feel _____ because I have always wanted to _____.

If I could change anything about myself right now, it would be _____ because then I would _____.

If I could do anything I wanted to do right now, it would be _____.

The only thing holding me back is _____.

You have just participated in a basic intuitive reading exercise. Don't be concerned if your answers don't seem to make sense right now. Occasionally we answer with a word or thought that seems unrelated to the statement. But think again. Do the words or thoughts that you wrote have any secondary significance to the statement? You will gain more insight into your responses as you move through this chapter. It's important to understand that without knowing it and with very little effort, you have just given yourself some simple answers to a few simple questions. These questions are:

What are you missing in your life right now that you hope to have someday? What do you want to feel right now that you are not feeling? What do you want to change about yourself? How would changing this also change your life? And, what do you need to change in your life or about yourself, so that you can spend more time doing what you really want to do? Can you believe you just gave yourself all those answers in less than five minutes? That's the intuitive process at work.

Intuition, which is information, answers, or messages that come to us in various forms, is readily available for the asking, but most of us are not skilled in working with our intuition. Intuition often comes to us voluntarily and either goes unrecognized or gets devalued. But whether it's a thought or an idea, a feeling, a touch, or a smell, you can often recognize intuitive input when you think or speak the following words:

I just had a feeling.
Something told me . . .
A voice inside said . . .
It just felt so right.
I had a gut feeling.
It was just a hunch I had.
I knew it was wrong from the beginning.

We all have these types of thoughts, but do we heed them or do we ignore them? Do we give them value or do we dismiss them? Do we pay attention to the messages, even when they're right in front of us?

Recognizing Intuitive Messages

You can be sure that intuition is at work when something you feel, hear, or see is too compelling to ignore. Have you ever felt that everything inside was telling you that you were going in the wrong direction or doing the wrong thing, but you ignored the feelings and signs and continued doing it anyway? Did you end up regretting it later? Most likely you did, and most likely, the regret could have been avoided. Possibly your intuition was sending you a message that your relationship wasn't healthy, but you were afraid of being alone, so you ignored the signs. Your intuition may have been telling you that a job you were about to take wasn't right for you, but you felt insecure about other options, so you took the job anyway.

We're extremely creative in finding subconscious ways to justify all the reasons why we should ignore our intuition. Often, we aren't even aware that we are doing this until we start paying attention. The trickiest part, though, is that our emotions, which are very compelling, often get in the way of our intuition. In most circumstances, the intuitive feeling comes first, and then the emotions follow. In some cases, our emotions may reinforce our intuition. In other cases, our emotions may justify our reasons why our intuition is incorrect, especially if we don't like what it's telling us. We need to practice recognizing our feelings in order to tune in to our intuition, but we must also learn to discern between intuitive feelings and emotions.

Like any other skill, intuition needs to be learned, and then it needs to be practiced. The more you practice tuning in to your intuition and learning to read it properly, the easier it becomes to trust your gut feelings, make your own decisions, and feel comfortable that the decision you made was probably the right one.

The Value of Intuition

If someone asked me today to name a single skill that has helped me define and realize my dreams and maintain control of my life, my kingdom, I would have to say it was intuition. There have been countless times when, despite the seemingly rational advice around me, listening to my inner feelings has saved my business and taken it to new and exciting levels, guided me in my professional career, helped me make difficult personal life decisions, helped me stay happily married and be a better parent, guided me in taking responsibility for my health or a family member's health, and helped me to maintain a strong spiritual base in my life.

The purposes of intuition are the following:

1. To provide you with more information about the concern at hand. Intuitive messages are wonderful sources of information that come from the best resource of all, your inner feelings and thoughts.

2. To help you make decisions more quickly and more confidently. You'll stop second-guessing your decisions and have more faith in the outcome.

3. To help you clarify your dreams and desires through the skill of Intuitive Visualization, which will be discussed in this chapter.

4. To allow you to get in touch with your core feelings about the situation you are pondering. In this busy, overstimulated world in which we live, it's sometimes hard to listen to our true feelings.

5. To get beyond your emotions and logic, both of which get in the way of taking risks and following your heart.

6. To use the skill of Intuitive Visualization to provide an intimate perspective that would be difficult, if not impossible, to reach otherwise.

Using your intuition on a regular basis will give you a sense of empowerment. You'll trust yourself and your feelings more, and you'll make confident decisions. You'll also have a new sense of patience and faith that things are working the way they should, regardless of outside appearances.

How to Work with Your Intuition

The following steps will help you become more familiar with the intuitive process:

1. *Open your mind.* Begin to believe in your ability to sense things. Open your mind to the possibility that you are sensory, that you are intuitive.

2. *Open your eyes.* Begin looking for clues, signs, and symbols that could have meaning in your life or in regard to a particular situation.

3. *Open your senses.* What do you smell, hear, feel, touch, and taste that might offer a clue? All of your senses offer the opportunity to acquire information, so how does a particular sensation address your concern?

4. *Pay attention.* You are receiving messages constantly. It's up to you to pay attention to your inner messages and the outer signs that surround you.

5. *Read the signs.* Often the signs are so obvious, they could knock you down. Yet they are worthless if you don't take a moment to interpret them.

6. *Add to your information database.* All the information bases, including intuitive messages, divine guidance, and synchronistic events, are resources to help you gain a better

understanding of the importance of trusting yourself and the flow of life.

The information resource of intuition, when taken seriously, can help you to improve your self-confidence and clarify your life's direction. As you begin to make better choices, you will acquire a sense of patience and understanding about the way life works.

Intuition and Divine Validation

Instinct is the nose of the mind.

—MADAME DE GIRARDIN

To illustrate the way intuition has worked in my life, I'd like to tell you about a "near death" experience I had not too long ago. It actually had nothing to do with physical death, but it had everything to do with the near death of my company, the Midwest Center for Stress and Anxiety. Had it not been for following my intuition, listening to my gut in an intense moment of pressure, my company would be gone as I write this book.

It took me sixteen years to build The Midwest Center, of which I'm extremely proud. As well as helping lots of people, it also has been my family's sole source of support and long-term security, not to mention that of the twenty or so employees on our staff, who helped build the company.

We had been getting such positive feedback from people who had successfully gone through the "Attacking Anxiety" program that the entire staff agreed it was time to expand. We wanted our program to be in every doctor's office, hospital, and

Employee Assistance Program around the country. Because we also wanted it to be available through insurance carriers and major health maintenance organizations (HMOs), we did extensive research, designed a concise business plan, and began to look for a business partner.

We approached a big player in the health care field. After convincing the company that there was a market for our product, we showed them how our business strategy could be implemented. Almost immediately, they offered us a deal that included tremendous distribution potential as well as their expertise and, of course, money, if we would partner with the company. It seemed like perfect timing. This company had deep pockets, great distribution channels, and strong relationships in our industry. On the surface, it appeared to be an offer we couldn't and probably shouldn't refuse.

In a defining meeting, my staff and I presented what we considered to be a fair business plan, which included an offering of part of our company. As the negotiations progressed, as we had subsequent meetings around the country and worked out possible joint venture options, events began to take a strange turn. Although our offer was clearly defined and generous, the other company kept requesting additional confidential information as to exactly how we would implement the project. The approach was starting to feel suspect, as if it was asking for more than it needed to know. This was my first sign.

As I began to "feel" uncomfortable, I started noticing representatives from the other company acting shrewd and condescending. This further caused me to sense a hidden agenda, and as time progressed, I had several dreams about control issues. My dreams didn't relate specifically to the players involved in the deal, but I saw them as possible signs related to the negotiations. In the meantime, my feelings of discomfort continued to escalate. While my board members, my corporate team, my confidantes, my advisers, and, especially, my most respected consultant and partner, my husband, David, were eagerly wanting to move forward, I was pulling back.

In direct opposition to my emotional desire to do this joint venture, my intuition was nagging at me to rethink the deal. This did not go over well with my board, and I could understand why. We had all worked hard toward our shared goal, and my associates were too quickly prepared to label my intuitive feelings as "overconcern," simply because they wanted the venture to happen so badly. Despite the pressure that my staff was putting on me, this particular deal continued to "feel" totally wrong to me—a hard thing to explain to an excited group of business associates who were pressing to move forward.

In a meeting that had been called specifically to clarify deal points, our potential partners surprised everybody but me. They had decided to play hardball, and they began the meeting with intimidation, attempting to devalue our stock. Then came another blow: if we didn't comply with everything they wanted, they threatened to steal our ideas and to implement them via another organization. The room was thick with tension. At one point, a member of their management team actually said to me, "Missy, you just don't get it. We are an eight-hundred-pound gorilla and you are a flea." In other words, they were threatening to eat us alive if we didn't cooperate. And, boy, did they look hungry! The red flags were flapping in the crosswind, but my team didn't see them because they were operating from a fear base.

When we broke for a brief conference, I quietly listened to my board members, who were all afraid we would be put out of business. When we walked back into the room, we could feel the other team's smug presumptuousness, thinking they had us over a barrel and were about to get everything they wanted. My board members flashed me stressful looks, and one of my consultants passed me a note that said, "Do the deal!" Even in the midst of intimidation and immense pressure, they still wanted to move forward.

I sat there overwhelmed and confused. I believed in my company, I believed in my board, and I believed in our vision. Now I had to get focused and decide if I believed in my intuition. Right there, in the midst of that high-pressure situation, I stopped, breathed, and scanned my body. My head hurt. My stomach was upset. My shoulders were so tight that it felt like someone was sitting on me, holding me down. There was a dark, heavy feeling in the room, which indicated negative energy to me. I heard a voice inside of me, which I now refer to as my "God voice," screaming, "WALK AWAY NOW!"

I had found clarity. I pushed away from the table and said, "We are not prepared to negotiate today. Please put your offer in writing and send it to us. We'll review it and get back to you." I stood up and walked out. No matter what they'd offered, and even if turning it down would have meant the end of our company, I simply knew at that moment that we should not do business with these people. They were far too negative and condescending, and it was obvious to me that they could not be trusted. For the first time, it was completely clear to me: our business was about our vision, a vision that started years ago, one that these other people obviously didn't share.

For months following my decision to walk away, the entire board thought that I had made a huge mistake. Each of them felt certain that I had blown a once-in-a-lifetime opportunity. It was painful for me to hear their opinions. We argued, we debated, but I held firm. We began to hear talk in the industry that the other company was moving forward with our ideas with someone else. It didn't change my mind. I would not work with these people at any price.

Time passed, and they did move forward with our ideas without us. It was a great relief to me, and quite affirming, when we heard that their attempts to implement our strategies in the marketplace had failed. In the following months, the rest of the industry realized that these people were not operating with integrity or good business practices. Soon, their corporate name started appearing all over the news in connection with dark business dealings and illegal actions. They were under daily investigation in every newspaper across the country; the purported giant was falling. We stood back and watched as one of the largest, fastest-growing health care companies of all time fell apart before our eyes.

In the end, everyone on my team admitted that if we had done the deal, we would have gone down with them. If I hadn't listened to my intuitive feelings and stayed firm in the face of intense pressure, we would be out of business today. What validation for one of the most difficult decisions I had ever made! I review this experience whenever I'm questioning my instincts.

Had I been afraid not to do the deal? Yes.

Had I feared for the future of our company when I walked away? You bet!

Did I have second thoughts about my decision at times? Of course.

Could I have been wrong? Yes. But that was a risk I was willing to take because the feelings were so strong.

Divine Signs and Validation

When you start recognizing divine signs, your decisions will come faster, you'll feel better about them, and you won't waste precious energy doubting yourself. Intuitive feelings aren't always that clear, though. In fact, the hardest thing about making a decision based on your intuition is that the messages often seem vague or mixed. Maybe you won't see the payoff until months or years down the road. The point is that you can't be one hundred percent sure of anything, and the waiting period for validation can be grueling. If you begin to look for signals that offer divine reinforcement, I guarantee you'll find them.

I've learned that when I hear mixed messages about a certain situation, it is often because I'm too emotionally involved to listen. If I pay close attention, I will hear a voice, to which I referred earlier as my "God voice." I can actually hear it speaking to me; in fact, there are times it even *screams* to be heard.

Shortly after I made the decision to walk away from the health care merger, I was forced to make another difficult decision. It was about whether or not I would agree to host a nationally syndicated talk show. Having my own show had been a lifelong goal and one of my biggest dreams, but something didn't feel right. The show seemed too tabloid, not a true or a positive reflection of my message. It was especially hard to make this decision because I had not yet received validation that walking away from the corporate partnership had been a smart move. That made walking away from another once-in-a-lifetime opportunity twice as challenging. After all, we had moved to Los Angeles to make these things happen.

I listened for intuitive input, but I seemed to be getting

mixed messages. In retrospect, I can see that my intense desire for the opportunity left me far too emotionally involved to be able to read the information correctly. Indeed, my "God voice" was speaking very clearly, but I subconsciously attempted to misinterpret it so that I could justify moving forward. In the end, the voice was too strong to ignore. Despite my desires, I had to acknowledge that it would be a bad move to host a show of this type; I simply had to walk away.

I immediately began second-guessing myself. *Was I going in the right direction? Was I making good decisions?* Everyone in the television industry had told me this talk show was an incredible opportunity. The money was big. The producer was big. Once again, in the face of something that looked like a dream come true, I declined the offer on the strength of an intuitive sign. Believe me, I was feeling down and confused. *Would these opportunities ever come again? Was I making the right choices?* I was exhausted from the confusion; I needed validation.

On the night that I turned down the show, I wanted to be silent and to think, so I sat in the spare bedroom in my house where there would be no interruptions. First, I prayed to God to continue to guide me, and then I spoke to my sister Donna. She and I had been very close until she passed away several years ago. Since her death, there had been a number of times when I'd communicated with her in my mind and got an immediate response, so I decided to try it again.

Donna, I said, *I'm a little confused and disillusioned. I felt I had to walk away from both of these opportunities, but it was really hard, and it still is. Now I'm questioning my judgment. Have I done the right things here? Is it going to come together for the good of all concerned? Please, if you can manage it, I need a sign immediately—*

well, at least by tomorrow. Then, attempting to put it out of my mind, I walked upstairs and went to bed.

The next day, when I got home from work, there was a messenger waiting at my door. He was holding a beat-up package, and when he saw me, he smiled. "Whew," he said, "I had a really hard time finding this place. Are you Lucinda Bassett?"

I nodded, looking a bit puzzled. My home was not a difficult one to find, but the package looked as if it had been dragged through the jungle.

"This is for you," he said, extending it toward me. I thanked him. When I walked inside and opened the package, I found a beautiful arrangement of pink and rose-colored silk flowers, tied up with a delicate silk ribbon. The enclosed note was from a woman named Laura who had gone through my "Attacking Anxiety" program and felt that the tapes had saved her life. She wrote, "I suddenly felt compelled to send you these flowers." She also had enclosed a heartwarming poem she had written to God, thanking Him for her recovery. At the end of her poem, she had written something that brought tears to my eyes: "Thank you for Lucinda Bassett. Her course has been my breath of life, CPR for the self I suffocated so long ago."

I laid the flowers on the piano. What an emotional moment! What validation that I was on the right path with my work. Suddenly, my son, Sammy, who was six at the time, came running into the room.

"Look, Sammy," I said. "A woman named Laura sent me these flowers. Aren't they beautiful?"

He stared at them with a strange look on his face. Then he walked closer to the floral arrangement and said, "Oh, Mommy, these aren't from her. They're from Aunt Donna."

I looked at him in amazement. "What did you say?"

"Aunt Donna sent these flowers, Mommy," he repeated. Then he ran out of the room, leaving me in awe. I was so overwhelmed by his comment that I had to sit down. He and I hadn't talked about Donna for quite some time. So what made Sammy think about her at that moment? Furthermore, he had no way of knowing that throughout our adult lives, Donna and I had always sent each other flowers in times of confusion or despair. She was gone now, but what Sammy said felt completely right. Donna had used this woman to send me a very clear message; and with the help of my child, I had gotten it. This was the "sign" I had asked for the night before! I had almost forgotten I'd even asked.

In that moment, I knew without a doubt that I had made the right decision to let go of both opportunities and to keep plugging away until something else felt totally right. I suddenly knew it would all come together.

Again, it's about making the right choices. When you are trying to build a life, one that involves achieving success and happiness and acquiring a sense of security and independence, it is easy to be drawn into the wrong situation simply because it looks good on the surface. This is an important time to use your intuitive resources to help guide your decisions and to keep your path clear.

Divine Guidance

Have you ever experienced divine guidance? Maybe it was someone you met, something you read, or an event that appeared to be a "coincidental" happening. The truth is there are divine clues all around us, and they often come to us when we don't even realize we're asking for them. For example, have you ever been thinking about a problem, only to turn on the radio or television and find something being discussed that related to your specific situation? You might have thought to yourself, "What a coincidence!" But I think coincidence has very little to do with it.

How many times have you been sitting in church when you realized that the minister was addressing your exact fear or worry? Have you ever met someone who affected your life in a way that seemed predestined, and you just knew she or he came into your life for a reason? Have you ever had a lifesaving experience where divine intervention seemed absolute? Have you ever heard yourself saying: "That's a sign" or "Someone must have been looking out for me" or "I must have a guardian angel." Whether we admit it or not, we all have experiences from time to time that we can't explain, and we receive signs every day that we don't even notice. Unfortunately, few of us pay attention to the signs, even when they are so obvious that they are literally smacking us over the head! But just think of what you can do with all that information once you start paying attention to it and know how to use it!

> *Intuition is a spiritual faculty and does not explain, but simply points the way.*
>
> —FLORENCE SCOVEL SHNN

Divine clues or messages often come without our asking for them. But when we do ask and watch for an answer, the results can be amazing. These signs can come in various forms. They may be symbols that grab your attention, or a particular object that was always there, but you suddenly notice it. Perhaps another person tells you something, or lyrics to a song you've heard a dozen times suddenly seem to be speaking to you directly. As opposed to your "God voice," which seems to derive from within, divine clues often seem to come from an outside source of information or a combination of outside data and intuitive messages.

A couple of years ago, I was in Tampa, Florida, on a business trip. In a conversation with my mother, I had learned that my cousin Nancy was a cancer patient in a hospice "somewhere" in the Clearwater/St. Petersburg area. After I was there for a day, I couldn't ignore a compelling feeling to go see Nancy, but I didn't know how to find her and neither did my mother. We knew she had remarried, but neither of us had seen or talked with her for a few years, and we didn't know her new last name.

I called around and eventually located the hospice where I thought she was staying. They informed me that a woman named Nancy, who would be about the right age, was a resident there. Because she was able to come and go with assistance, she wasn't in at that moment. For the next few days I tried to reach her but with no luck. I nearly gave up. Then, one afternoon, I decided to run out to the store for a few odds and ends.

For some reason, as I was leaving the hotel room, I grabbed the address of the hospice and put it in my purse. As I was driving, I thought back to when my first book, *From Panic to Power*, came out and how excited all my relatives had been when they heard about it. A family member had written a book! Everyone was so proud. At that moment, I wished I had a copy of my book with me, imagining that Nancy might like to see it, if I ever did manage to connect with her. I was in a nearly deserted shopping plaza when suddenly I spotted a new and used book store. *What are my chances of finding a copy of my book in there?* I thought. After all, the book had been out for two and a half years, and I was in the middle of nowhere. Unable to ignore a compelling feeling to park and walk to the store, I could hardly believe my eyes when right there in the window I saw a brand new copy of my book in hardback. When I picked up the book, it was as if I heard it saying, *This is a sign. Go see Nancy right now.* I purchased the book, pulled out the address from my wallet, and asked for directions.

Within the hour, I was sitting with Nancy at the hospice, my book in her hands, while we reminisced about family reunions at Grandma's house, recalling the sound of mourning doves when we played in her overgrown backyard. We talked, we laughed, we cried. Most important for both of us, we connected. With the help of the divine sign of my book showing up and hearing my God voice, my intuition had guided me to see her. When she died, I felt blessed to have spent that time with her, a gift that I might not have received if I hadn't paid attention to the obvious signs guiding me.

As you can see, the rewards that often come when you pay attention to divine intervention can be wonderful. The signs, however, aren't always as clear as they were with Nancy. Sometimes they are vague, and sometimes they are clear but then you interpret them incorrectly.

Not too long ago, one of my clients was confused by a divine clue. He had been working on a business venture, and he really wanted it to happen. After meeting with one of the primary players, he and his business partner went to a restaurant to grab a quick bite and talk about the deal. They both felt good about the meeting, but as they were leaving the restaurant, something happened that concerned him. He began to hear the theme song from the movie, *Titanic*, and he felt a tremendous wave of sadness. He was so overwhelmed that he called me that afternoon and told me what had happened.

"Do you think my feelings mean this business deal is dying?" he asked.

During the past few months of working with his intuition, he had experienced some significant intuitive episodes, so he had learned to take these types of feelings seriously. "I don't know, Lucinda," he said. "I felt the meeting went very well, and so did my partner. But why am I feeling this sadness, as if there is a death coming?" I told him I wasn't sure, but that it was good that he paid attention. I believed it did have meaning, but I wasn't sure in relationship to what. It was good to hear that both he and his partner felt the meeting went well. I suggested that he remain patient and let the answer unfold.

The next morning, he awakened to the news that a very close friend had died. She had been struggling for a long time, and he had made various visits to her home during her illness. She was a powerful woman. Her presence was huge in his life, and they were closely connected. He had indeed felt a death the night before, but it was the death of a person, not his business deal. Looking back, he could see that the *Titanic* theme song was representative of his friend's strength as a person and of her death. His initial feelings about the business deal were correct. It moved forward successfully.

I want to make it clear that neither divine clues nor intuition are the whole picture. Pay attention to your feelings, recognize and observe your intuition, watch for and be aware of divine clues, but don't use any one of these as your sole source of information. Consider all aspects of something by reviewing the data you receive along the way. See how it all fits together. Then, you can make an informed decision with the help of both physical and intuitive messages.

Intuitive Visualization

Today, intuition is considered by many professionals to be a highly respected part of decision making. Psychologists, doctors, scientists, and others are beginning to recognize the power of intuition and the significance of synchronicity in our lives. There is a great deal of information available about how to cultivate optimal states of consciousness. Many experts believe that when we master the skill of reading our intuition, we will be able to perceive certain signs as answers to our questions. Judging from my personal experience, I have to agree. Practicing my intuitive skills has helped me to make better decisions and to clarify reasons for confusing occurrences, and has allowed me to better define my life's direction.

Beginning Intuitive Visualization

Here is a simple beginning Intuitive Visualization exercise to help you tap into the intuitive response process:

STEP 1: Find a quiet place to sit or lie down. Think of a situation that is concerning you right now, something for which you want some "inside information." Take a few minutes to listen to your breath in order to become inwardly focused, highly tuned to your senses and feelings. When your breathing has become calm, ask yourself a particular question about your situation. Be as specific as possible.

Here are some examples of direct, specific questions:

Should I take this job as office manager?

Why am I afraid to write this book?

Should I buy this particular home right now?

Why isn't this relationship working?

Should I follow this dream?

What is the delay about?

Is this the right opportunity for me?

Where will I be in relation to my career three years from now?

STEP 2: Now sit back, close your eyes, and let yourself relax. As thoughts enter your mind, examine them and then gently let them go, giving equal time and importance to any messages you receive. Give yourself plenty of time. If thoughts don't come right away, don't get discouraged. Maybe your mind is too busy at this moment, or maybe all the circumstances aren't clearly defined yet and the answer is still forming. At some point, a picture will start to form in your mind, which can provide you with tons of information.

STEP 3: Now ask yourself: *What picture has come into my mind? How could it possibly relate to my question?* Write it all down in detail. Ask yourself: *What colors do I see? What objects? What memories does this bring to mind? Is there something in this picture that could be a clue to my question?*

Remember that intuition is a sensory experience; so pay attention to your senses. What's going on around you? Are there words in your mind or a name perhaps? Is there a sound from the outside that has entered your space? Can you hear your "God voice"? Does something feel right or wrong? What are you touching and what could it represent? What do you taste or smell at this moment that might offer a clue?

STEP 4: Now tune in to your body. How does it feel when you ask the question? Are you anxious, or are you excited? Are you uncomfortable, or are you relaxed? This sensory input is the raw material for intuitive messages.

STEP 5: Open your eyes, write it all down. Sometimes the pictures in your mind or the messages you receive may appear to have little to do with the question or the actual situation you may be pondering. Write them down anyway. Don't disregard anything. If you allow some time for the big picture to unfold, you'll see how each detail relates to the answer for which you are searching.

Let me give you an example of this exercise working in the life of one of my clients recently. She and her husband share a dream to live in a house by the ocean someday. She loves houses with character and old-world charm, so something older with a garden and mature trees would appeal to her. This isn't a luxury she and her husband feel they can afford right now, but it is something toward which they are working. Just for fun and future information, she decided to try out her new skills and check her intuition for an answer.

She was on her way to a meeting at an office she had never been to before when she decided to give it a try. She parked, closed her eyes, and asked: *Will we live in a house by the ocean within the next five years?* She pondered the question for a moment and then noticed that her mouth tasted of salty crackers. She got out of the car and walked into the office with the question still fresh in her mind. She sat down in the waiting area, closed her eyes, and asked the question again. The first thing she noticed when she opened her eyes was a beautifully painted, aged, yellow wall in the office. This indicated to her that their possible future home would have aged yellow stucco on the outside. Next, her eyes focused on the lushness outside the windows, and then she noticed deep blue water out in the distance. This signified to her that the house would be surrounded with lush green plants and trees and that it would be by the water. As she looked down, her eyes were drawn to a magazine that had the year 2001 written on its cover, which indicated to her that they would probably make the move in that year. She wrote all of this down. By the way, these were not visual connections that came to her attention before the exercise. The fact that her mouth tasted of salty crackers was particularly interesting, as she took it to signify that the house would be by the ocean.

Does she know for a fact that this will happen? Of course not. But it was fun to do the exercise and she said that somehow it felt right, offering her a sense of calm resolve that all their hard work would pay off someday.

Intuitive Visualization Storyboarding

We practice the skill of Intuitive Visualization by simply allowing the mind to free-fall. Once we let new ideas and thoughts take form without the invasion of our emotions, we can create a storyboard from our intuitive pictures. Then we can get some insight into a specific situation.

The following process, which I call Intuitive Visualization Storyboarding, can help you in all areas of your life, from business to relationships, to health, to raising your children. It consists of three steps:

STEP 1: *Sit in a quiet space where you won't have any interruptions.* Take a deep breath, clear your mind, and close your eyes. Continue to inhale and exhale, allowing your breath to find its own natural rhythm. Slowly watch the mind chatter recede into the background. When you feel calm and quiet, start to envision your mind as a clear slate, an empty storyboard about to be filled up with your personal story. You can have as many picture frames in a storyboard as you like, but for simplicity and direction, start with four separate frames inside your storyboard. The first frame, or picture, will be in the top left-hand corner, the second in the top right-hand corner, the third in the bottom left, and the fourth in the bottom right.

STEP 2: *Compose a direct question about your concern.* The more specific your question is, the better. Remember to be "time specific" also. For example, you might ask: *Will I be promoted in the next year?* Gently keep your mind focused on that exact question, inviting the thoughts to enter the forefront of your mind. Don't look for answers. Just keep your mind and body relaxed, and, with closed eyes, watch the movie in your head. Your mind is now ready to begin filling the storyboard. Ask yourself what is going on in the first frame of your storyboard. Are there other people? Is there activity? What do you see? What is happening in the second, then in the third, and finally in the fourth frame of your storyboard? The pictures you see in your storyboard are all different scenes of the story. In fact, they might not seem related to each other or to the question. But even if you can't make the connections right away, trust that each exposure is an integral part of a related situation and that, eventually, it will all come together to answer your question in some way—so no editing!

STEP 3: As the frames fill up and your complete storyboard begins to fill up, take notes. Let the pictures flow naturally, and don't worry if you think you're manipulating your mind to see what you want to see. You can't really manipulate it, because whatever appears is there for a reason, even if you're helping it along. So take mental note of any pictures that pop up. (You can make written notes when you open your eyes at the end of the exercise.) As time goes on, the more you analyze your storyboard and observe your notes, the more it will all come together to answer your question.

What are the hidden messages here that relate to your specific question? What are the pros and cons of the situation? As you think them through, notice how your body is responding. Do you have a headache? Do you feel tense? Do you feel a sense of dread or skepticism? Or do you feel excitement and joy? Take the information as a clue.

Here is an example of the storyboard exercise working in someone's life. A young woman named Marilyn with whom I was working decided to try this exercise to help clarify her career direction. She asked if within the next two years she would be getting a managerial position. In the first frame of her storyboard, she saw confusion and chaos. This made her feel anxious and concerned. In the second frame, she saw an office that suggested a sense of power. In the third frame, she saw herself in a conference room conducting a meeting. In the fourth frame of her storyboard, she saw herself surrounded by professional people and lots of activity.

She took this reading to mean that she would get the management position in her company, but she didn't understand the first frame. Then things took an unexpected turn. Her company went through some changes, and she had to find another job. For a couple of months, she felt confused and insecure. She thought she had experienced a "false" intuitive reading. As time passed, she got a new job; and a year later, she was promoted to manager. One day, she had a powerful déjà vu experience when she was sitting in the conference room with her co-workers. She suddenly knew that this moment had happened before. Then she remembered that this was the exact scene in the storyboard intuitive exercise she had done a year earlier.

Had she trusted her intuitive messages, she might have saved herself from the worry and insecurity involved in changing jobs. She would have had more confidence in herself and her abilities, and she would have had faith that her life was going in the right direction.

Here is another fun and insightful exercise that involves Intuitive Visualization.

STEP 1: Take a moment to *write down a specific question* to which you would like an immediate answer.

STEP 2: Clear your mind, relax your breathing, and close your eyes. *Think about the question you have just written down.* Ponder it for a few minutes.

STEP 3: Open your eyes. *What is the first object that you see?* What single object are you looking at right now? Describe it in detail in a written paragraph, no matter what it is.

Believe it or not, your description of this particular object just answered your question in some way. Your job is to simply evaluate your paragraph. Let me give you an example. Shortly after I walked away from the talk show opportunity, I was wondering if, in fact, I was ever destined to have a successful television talk show. This was something for which I had been working diligently; but, so far, my efforts had not produced the desired results. I closed my eyes and asked a direct question: *Am I going to find significant success hosting a talk show that's representative of what I do?*

When I opened my eyes, I was staring at a large clay pot that was standing upright on the floor in the corner of the room. I marveled at the roundness of it and how its shades of gray became lighter in color with each ascending layer. As I continued to analyze the pot, I noticed two handles placed at the top of both sides. The sturdiness of the handles and the way they were positioned indicated that the pot could be lifted high. The opening to the pot was quite large, while the base was small. I wrote down my description of the pot and then proceeded to interpret its relationship to my question.

Considering this object as my intuitive symbol, I began by determining that the pot, as a whole, was me. I saw the roundness as the circular movement of life. The pot stood upright, with a very large opening toward the sky, which I translated as my openness to allow an abundance of opportunities into my life. I interpreted the grayness as the way I began my life—with lots of fear and darkness. The layers that progressively lightened as they moved upward represented the way my life has lightened up with the work I've done, both on myself and with others. The handles at the sides of the pot indicated to me that with help I can be lifted very high and that, in fact, I will reach great heights. And yet, the relative smallness of the base reminded me that there are times when I feel so vulnerable I could tip over quite easily. On the whole, however, the pot was open and upright, the way I like to envision my heart and my career path. I took the answer to be a yes, that I would get what I wanted in time. I just needed to be aware of my vulnerability, to surround myself with uplifting people, and the opportunities would be abundant and available.

You may be wondering how I knew that I was interpreting the signs correctly. I didn't, but you'll find as I did that the more you practice the exercise and see it as a sort of game, the easier it will be to spot the clues and interpret them. Don't forget the importance of writing them down. Then if things turn out the way you've predicted, it's a wonderful validation. As with all intuitive exercises, it's important to keep in mind that nothing is one hundred percent certain. Intuition and divine signs are sources of information to add to your database.

These Intuitive Visualization exercises can be very effective in helping you fine-tune your intuition skills, but remember that many of these signs and messages come to us on a daily basis without effort. We just need to start paying attention and learn how to read them properly.

Misinterpreting Negative Feelings

I suggest you take a moment and think back on times in your life when you made bad choices. Now list them on a piece of paper, and beside each one, write how it affected you in your life, both in the short term and the long term. Review the list and think back about any signs you may have received that were telling you to go in a different direction. Perhaps the signs were too subtle to recognize. Perhaps they were obvious, but you chose to ignore them. Was your decision made from an emotional base? Was it made out of fear? Can you see now that listening more carefully to these signs and getting more information might have changed the outcome?

We need to consider all our signs and feelings, but because negative thinking feeds on itself, dwelling on negativity will ultimately color your ability to recognize the real message. When you interpret this negative type of thinking as an intuitive message instead of reading it for what it truly is—an expression of your fear—the negative thinking can go on and on, making it impossible to read your intuition correctly. Remember, fear is an emotion, intuition is not.

One of the most common questions I am asked is: "How do you know whether your anticipation of something bad happening is an intuitive message or simply your fear?" Sometimes it's hard to be sure. This is why it's so important to be honest about your emotions. First, ask yourself which came first—the intuitive feeling or the fear? Then ask yourself if you're reacting to an emotion or to a true message or sign. For example, I worked with a client once who had an extreme fear of flying. But there was a business trip she could no longer avoid, so she had to fly.

She was scared to death and felt certain her plane would crash. When I helped her look more closely at the situation, she realized that she was reacting to an emotional fear base. She was not experiencing an intuitive sign. In fact, when she deliberately did an Intuitive Visualization exercise about the trip, she actually saw the sky and the clouds, she heard relaxing music in the background, and she saw herself at her business destination, having fun. This made her feel much better and actually helped her take the trip with confidence.

It is important to know yourself well. Are you someone who tends to anticipate the worst? Do you second-guess yourself, expecting failure, filling your thoughts with the "what-ifs" of life? If so, do you see how your negative thinking affects your ability to read your intuition properly? Acknowledging this is half the battle, and using the skills you have learned in this book will help you to change these negative thought patterns.

Synchronistic Events

Many of the experiences I have shared with you in this chapter combine intuitive experiences with synchronistic events. According to Jungian psychology, a *synchronistic event* is one that takes place at a transitional moment in one's life, defying a simple cause-and-effect explanation. I am a firm believer in synchronicity. I don't believe all synchronistic events to be life changing, but I do believe they often lead people in directions they unknowingly need to go. The event is personally meaningful or symbolic, but remember: one person's life-transforming event may be another person's banality.

A Lesson in Synchronicity

My niece Jennifer had an experience that taught her a lot about intuition, synchronicity, and the confusion that can surface when fear and what-if thinking are misinterpreted as messages. Jennifer had nearly completed four years of college when she applied to several dental schools, including one in Louisville, Kentucky, the city where she was raised. She had enjoyed growing up in Louisville until her mom was diagnosed with cancer. At that point, their lives became filled with pain and turmoil. Her parents decided to sell their home and move near a large clinic in Florida so her mom could get better care until she still died. While Jennifer was finishing college in Florida, her dad and sister moved back to Louisville. Now, Jennifer was being asked to come to Louisville for an interview. Although her father and sister lived there, Jennifer was afraid to return to the city where she had so many painful memories.

Then the signs began. When she first applied to various schools, she had jokingly told me that the only way she'd ever attend school in Louisville, her hometown, would be if it were the only school that called her. Even though Jennifer is an excellent student with wonderful grades and great credentials, Louisville was the only school that responded and wanted to set up an interview. During the weeks before the interview, it seemed that everyone Jennifer met was from Louisville. Then, out of the blue, her best friend from high school, whom she hadn't heard from since she'd left Louisville, called her. Small signs were beginning to become more obvious, but she still found it difficult to tap into her intuition or even to acknowledge the messages, through such deep pain.

When the time came for the trip to Louisville, she was reluctant and frightened. "What if I go back there and it brings up all kinds of bad feelings?" Jennifer said to me. "I don't really want to go to school there anyway." I understood her reluctance. At the same time, I knew she had to go back, at least for the interview, because she needed to address her feelings about the town and her pain. Perhaps more importantly, she hadn't spent much time with her father and sister since her mother died, and I felt they all needed to be together. I knew that her worry and fear were not allowing the right messages to get through, but I also knew it had to be her decision, so I kept quiet.

Immediately after her dad called to help schedule her trip, she called me, emotionally distraught. "I heard my mom's favorite song on the radio last night," she said. "My insides are telling me to go, but I'm afraid. What if I hate it back there? I don't think I'm 'supposed' to go that school." She was confused and anxious.

"Jennifer," I said, "listen to your heart, not your fear. You can't keep running from the past. You can find a ton of what-ifs about the situation, but the truth is, you're giving your negative thoughts way too much power. If you allow your fear to run you, you'll never have a chance to get to the real answer. So take it one step at a time.

"Go on the interview, see how it feels once you get there. Then you can make an informed decision."

She booked the flight. Once in Louisville, while she sat waiting for her interview in the outer office, another song came on the radio that reminded her of her mother. Then, during her tour of the campus, something inside her shifted. She began to feel that she was in the right place, and her fears disappeared.

Suddenly, she absolutely knew this was where she would go to school. A month later, she called to tell me she had been accepted. "Eighteen hundred kids applied and only eighty got in!" she announced with joy. "I just knew on the day of the interview that I was going to get in."

I wasn't surprised. I'm so glad Jennifer was able to cut through the what-ifs, take a risk, and get to the real answers, all by herself. It could have turned out differently. She could have let her fear and what-if thinking guide her in the wrong direction. In the worst case, she might not have attended dental school at all, spending a lifetime of regret, justifying why she never would have made it anyway.

Needless to say, her father and sister are happy that the family will be reunited at a time when they all really need each other. I absolutely believe it was predestined for Jennifer to end up in Louisville.

Listening to Your Inner Voice

I am certain there have been times in your life when you just knew something was supposed to be. My husband, David, says to this day that when we met eighteen years ago, there were "lightning bolts." He just knew we would be lifelong partners. On the night we met, he told my mother we would marry someday. She thought he was crazy, but he knew there was something powerful going on. So did I. When he held me in his arms, I felt I was finally home.

After studying intuition, divine guidance, and synchronicity and seeing them work in my life and in the lives of other people, I have come to believe that there are no coincidences. I see that a synergy connects all things and that these powerful resources are always there. Sometimes they're hidden, sometimes they're right at the surface, and each individual must decide to tap into them or to ignore them. The choice is up to you. All you have to do is open your mind to the thoughts and ideas that come to you. Open your eyes to the signals and signs that are all around you. And above all else, open your heart to the incredible sources of power that are available to all of us, bringing us success, health, abundance, and love. Your intuition is a wonderful gift, so why not utilize it as information that comes from the most reliable resource of all—you.

11

MIRACLES, PRAYER, AND FAITH

Mir·a·cle (mir'e-kel) 1. An event that seems impossible to explain by natural laws and so is regarded as supernatural in origin or as an act of God. 2. One that excites admiration and awe: wonder.

WEBSTER'S NEW WORLD DICTIONARY

Desperate for a Miracle

I find overnight flights exhausting, and this one was no exception. I couldn't sleep because of a nagging feeling that my mother was in trouble. As I mentioned at the beginning of Chapter 10, my mother was not doing well, and I insisted her doctor put her in the hospital. I was on my way home on the red-eye. After I landed in Detroit, it was a two-hour drive from the airport to the small hospital in Ohio where my mom had been admitted

262

the previous afternoon. I had agreed to pick up my brother Gary on my way through Toledo. As I pulled into his driveway, he was pacing at the front door. I knew something was wrong.

"Mom's in trouble. They think she's in a coma. They don't think she's going to make it," he said, trembling and holding back the tears. I panicked. "No! This can't be! I just talked with her on the phone last night before I got on the plane. I told her I was coming home. I didn't get to see her! She can't die! The doctor said it wasn't that serious. She can't die!" I began to cry. The drive to the hospital was filled with emotion and fear. What if I didn't get there in time? I felt helpless. Gary had his cell phone, so I called the hospital. She was still alive. I then called my medical director and good friend, Dr. Phil Fisher, and told him what I knew. "Call me as soon as you get to the hospital," he said.

When we entered the intensive care unit, the doctor and our brother Michael came to meet us. "I'm so sorry," said the doctor. "She was such a lovely woman."

I looked at him with fear and anger. "What do you mean . . . 'was'? She's not gone yet! What exactly happened last night? What is the diagnosis?" I demanded as we rushed through the halls toward the intensive care unit.

"Well, we're not sure" he proceeded with caution. "We're running some tests but it doesn't look good. She probably had a heart attack or a stroke." He paused and looked away in what seemed to be a state of embarrassment. "She's probably not going to make it, and if she does, she will have severe problems."

"What do you mean?" I asked.

"Well, she could be paralyzed or severely mentally impaired. It's hard to say, but she's completely nonresponsive right now.

I'm so sorry," he said, shaking his head and walking away. Obviously, he had written her off.

"Mom, it's me," I cried through my tears. "It's me, Cindy," I said, picking up her lifeless hand. All of a sudden her legs began to move, flailing a bit. "Well, she's obviously not paralyzed, she's not comatose, and she's not going to die!" I said with renewed hope as I headed for the phone. I knew it was time to take action. My God voice was telling me to get her out of there fast. She needed to be in a big, experienced medical center that could deal with this type of thing. Within the next few minutes, I talked with Dr. Fisher and some friends of mine at a large hospital an hour away. My brothers and I had a brief discussion, and within the hour she was being transported via ambulance to the hospital. Following the ambulance in my car, I was praying. "Please, God, don't take her from us. Dad is gone, our brother David is gone (he died fourteen years ago), our sister Donna is gone. Please don't take Mom yet. I need her." I was desperate, heartbroken, and exhausted.

The next few days were touch and go, as she lay in the intensive care unit, virtually unresponsive. There were tubes and machines everywhere. I didn't leave her side. My brother Gary was singing to her and holding her hand. My brother Michael was gently stroking her forehead. She was surrounded by intense love. Michael and I had gone into the waiting area to see our aunt, who had just arrived. All of a sudden Gary came running out of the ICU. "Mom just opened her eyes!" he exclaimed. We all ran in excitedly. There she was, looking at us! What a wonderful, glorious moment!

"Mom, can you hear us?" I said. She nodded. "Do you know it's us, Cindy, Gary, and Michael?" Again she nodded. She

looked drugged, confused, and exhausted, but she acknowledged us. Then she closed her eyes.

With each day, she seemed to get a bit more responsive as I
set up camp by her side. I simply wasn't leaving until I knew she
was out of danger. Gary and Michael and their families were
there constantly, offering love, support, and constant prayer. We
sang to her, told her jokes, and told her how much fun we were
going to have when she got better. Although she had a tube
down her throat, she managed a smile. She had been such a
great mother to all of us, such a source of pleasure and inspira-
tion. We weren't going to lose her now.

Finally things were calming down. The doctors still weren't
sure what had happened, but they suspected a severe stroke.
They didn't want to move her for more tests until she was more
stable. She had been in intensive care for four days now, and I
had not left her side. I desperately needed to shower and lie
down in a real bed. It was 11 P.M., and everyone, including my
brothers, had gone home. Mom appeared to be doing okay, so I
decided to take the hospital up on their offer to use a room
down the hall to rest.

"Call me if anything changes," I said to the nurse on duty.
She assured me that she would. At 3 A.M. that morning, the
phone in my room rang. It was the nurse and she was very upset.
"Your mom is not responding. Her blood pressure is dropping
rapidly. I've called her doctor," she said in a controlled state of
concern. She had grown fond of her, and I could tell she was
worried. I rushed to my mom's side.

"Mom, please, don't leave us now," I pleaded in desperation.
My tears were falling on her chest as I bent over her motionless
body. "Mom, I need you . . . don't leave me," I cried. Right then

the hospital chaplain entered the room. "What are you doing here?" I asked.

"I am here to give your mom her last rites," he responded, matter-of-factly. "Well, I'm sorry, but she's not going anywhere. Please go. I'll let you know if we need you." He walked out of the room, a bit thrown. My response sounded abrupt, even to me, but I was not prepared to let her die, not then. It just didn't "feel" as if she was supposed to die.

At that moment, I felt a sense of complete desperation through to my soul. I picked up her hands and began to pray. I prayed as I have never heard myself pray before. "Dearest God, dear Jesus, please, let your love come through my body and heal my mother. Dearest Lord, hear my prayer and heal this woman. Let her be a testimony to your strength and love." My prayers were intense and focused and continued for a time span that I cannot measure. It was as though I was completely lost in the moment, and we were totally surrounded by God's love. We were cocooned in a blanket of warmth, alone but not alone. It was like nothing I had ever experienced, and yet on some level, I knew exactly what I was doing. I was asking for a miracle, plain and simple.

I placed my hand on her forehead and continued praying. All of a sudden, my mother's entire body jerked, as if she had received some kind of shock. It scared me so much that I jumped back a few feet. *Oh, my God,* I thought to myself. *I've killed her!* I stood exhausted and frightened and just stared at her. Mom gently opened her eyes. My eyes swelled with tears as I softly took her hand. "Mom, Mom, can you hear me?" She did not respond, instead she cocked her head and stared over my left shoulder. Her gaze was so compelling that I turned around to see "who" or what she was staring at, but there was no one there. She continued to look over my shoulder. "Mom, what are you looking at?" I asked gently. Right then, the nurse came running in, followed by a doctor. "She seems to be coming back!" the nurse said in amazement as she began various procedures.

At that moment, Mom had a look on her face that I'll never forget. It was as though she understood something. It was so completely peaceful.

She continued to stabilize. My brothers came in, unaware of what had happened in the wee hours of the morning. They attempted to reassure me, but they hadn't been through what I just experienced. The doctor came in and said they would be running tests for the next few hours to determine what had happened earlier and to try to determine what was wrong with her. I decided to use this time to go take a much-needed shower. As I finished, the phone rang. It was the vice president of the hospital, who was a good friend of mine. "Look, Lucinda, I wanted to be the one to tell you this. It doesn't look good. They are running the tests now, but they believe she has encephalitis on the brain or brain-stem damage. If she does survive, she will probably have severe brain damage. I just thought you should be prepared," he said with compassion.

I was devastated. How could this be happening? It was all such a bad dream. I was so overwhelmed and afraid. This was Mom, my best friend, my last woman connection in my immediate family since my sister had died. This was the woman who shared my joys and sorrows, the one I called when something wonderful was happening, the one who offered support and compassion when things went wrong. I was lost. I wanted to call her to talk to her about what I was going through. She would know what to say to comfort me, but *she* was what I was going through. I walked down the corridor to the hospital chapel. As I entered, I found myself cursing God. "How could you do this to me?" I cried. "I can't lose her. Please, take . . . take something else, take my company, but don't take my mother. Please," I begged.

I'm not sure why I said that, and I can't believe I did. There is certainly no comparative value there. But it just came out. It was as if on some level I could trade something that really meant a lot to me, for something that meant a whole lot more. I am not sure how long I was in the chapel, but I know my heart was heavy. I didn't know what else to do. I have never felt so alone in my life.

As I entered the lobby where my brothers and their wives were waiting for the results of Mom's tests, I collapsed in my brother Gary's arms, sobbing. "Hey, what's wrong, sis? Come on, she's going to be okay."

"What do you mean?" I asked, surprised by his positive response.

"The doctor just came out and said they didn't find anything significant. They aren't sure, but they think she had a mild stroke," he said, trying to comfort me. I sat there in total and complete amazement.

As the days progressed, she continued to improve. The doctors were completely baffled. Initially, because of the severity of her symptoms and her condition, they were sure she had suffered a severe heart attack or severe stroke, and they even medicated her for encephalitis on the brain, just in case. But the tests all came back negative. The only thing that showed up was the "possibility" of a "slight" stroke and seizure. Her neurologist was dumbfounded. "In twenty-five years of practice, I have never seen anything like this. She was in very bad shape. I have never seen anyone recover this well from something so devastating."

There were concerns of her ever being to swallow again, but I knew she would. There were concerns of her being able to talk again or walk again, but I knew she would. At one point, one of her doctors shook his head in disbelief at her recovery. "She is doing unbelievably well," he said. "But it is doubtful she'll walk again. Don't hope for a miracle." But I knew we had already gotten one.

As the weeks passed and she began to heal, the tubes were removed from her throat and transferred to her stomach. I'll never forget that day. My brother's wife, Donna, walked in as Mom tried to speak after the tube was removed from her throat. "Tubeless in Toledo," Donna said, and we all laughed.

Finally, after a few days, she began to talk softly, almost a whisper. On one particular afternoon, she pulled me aside. "There's something I need to tell you . . . privately," she said softly. When everyone left the room, I sat by her side to listen. "Something happened to me while I was very sick that I need to tell you about." Her eyes began to fill with tears. She was overwhelmed with emotion, as I have never seen her in my life. She took a deep breath as if she was afraid to say what she was about to tell me. "It's all right, Mom," I reassured her. "What is it?"

"I didn't want to tell anyone else, because I thought they would think I was crazy or imagining things," she said, still quite emotional. "But I know I didn't imagine this. It was very real. I'm not sure when it was, but . . ." she drew a deep breath and began to cry softly, "I saw my guardian angel. It was the most beautiful thing I have ever seen." She paused as if seeing it again for the first time. "First there was this brilliant light. It was so bright I wanted to turn away, but it was so compelling that I couldn't," she continued. "It was such an overwhelming feeling of love. I just had to tell you," she said through her tears. I was so moved by her emotion that I cried with her. "Mom, when did you see this?" I asked, wondering if that might have been what she was looking at that night in the intensive care unit when she kept looking over my shoulder.

"I don't know," she said, trying to remember. "I think I was awake when I saw it, though. It was golden with wings and I heard the sound of . . . I heard wings." And then she made the shape of wings with her hands. "Did it frighten you?" I asked. "No, not at all. It was there to comfort me. It made me feel safe," she said, relieved to have shared the experience.

My mother is an intelligent, practical, no-nonsense woman. She is spiritual, she is a Christian, and she believes in God, but she had never experienced anything like that before. And she remembers it vividly to this day. I couldn't help wondering if the angel was our companion in the intensive care that night, the source of spiritual strength that helped me to pray so profoundly for her life, the vision that caused her to gaze over my left shoulder with such intensity and peacefulness.

It was a long, hard road to recovery, but I am happy to say Mom is totally fine now. Just recently, she and I attended my niece Lori's graduation. We took walks on the beach, shared morning cappuccinos, and even "crashed" a wedding reception in our hotel to dance to a few songs. You'd never know by looking at her that she went through such a horrible ordeal.

Be Careful What You Ask For

Another powerful and an amazing validation of the power of God in my life was what happened to my company as my mother recovered—it began to fall apart. Before she got sick, I had three big deals in the works, I was selling products on QVC (a cable shopping network), and my book, *From Panic to Power*, had just been released and was doing well. Things were going great. As my mother started to recover, things in my company started to disintegrate. At first, I didn't even make the connection; but then I remembered my prayer and I was literally overwhelmed by it. One thing after another seemed to fall apart before my eyes. No matter how hard I tried or how right it all was, nothing was working. In between trips to New York and Philadelphia, I would swing by the rehab unit in Toledo to visit Mom. She was doing great. I was so happy.

As several months passed, nothing I did seemed to affect the downward spiral of my business. The product wasn't selling well on QVC, the book wasn't selling as well as expected, and new business deals all fell through. One Sunday in church, I sat thinking about Mom's recovery and the prayer I had prayed in the chapel that day. *Did I really bargain with God? Did he give my mother her life in exchange for my company?* And if he did, that's fine, I'm so happy to have her back. I needed to know, though, so I could move on if that was what I was supposed to do. It may sound a bit far-fetched, but it was too coincidental to ignore. I made an appointment to speak with my minister.

When I walked into his office that day, I was devastated from yet another business failure. He sat and listened as I told him what happened to my mother, and I explained about the prayer. "Did I bargain with God? Did he take my company away? I mean if he did, it's okay, but I just need to know." I was confused and sad and extremely humbled. "I can't believe he would take it away, though, because we do so much good, we make a difference. If my company's not there, a lot of people won't get the help they need," I said, searching his face for an answer.

"With God as Your Partner, You Can Win!"

He took my hands in his and said, "Lucinda, you didn't bargain with God; you bargained with the negative side of the universe, whatever you want to call it. God didn't take it away, but God can help you get it back. If you stand firm and let God be your partner and have faith, you will be stronger than the negative energy that you are fighting, and you can win." Then he said, "If God would have wanted to take it away, there would be nothing you could do about it. But God doesn't bargain." I didn't know if he was right—after all he is only human, just like me. But at that moment I needed some insight. I needed to make sense of it all. For the first time in my life, I understood what "the fear of God" meant. If God decides to take something away, it's a done deal. But God didn't take this away, and God and I could get it back. This was a powerful revelation.

I know this may all sound a bit corny, but it was profound for me and very real. I immediately started praying and thinking positively. I felt a very strong sense of empowerment and faith. I just knew things were going to be fine. I felt like a warrior who had the most powerful of soldiers on his side. I couldn't lose. I just knew I had nothing to fear. I told David what the minister said, and he prayed with me. My daughter, Brittany, had made a beautiful quilt at school that I had purchased at a fundraiser that week. Brittany suggested we all say a family prayer together, and she suggested we sit on the quilt to pray. It was such a tender moment as we prayed together as a family on that beautiful little quilt. I'll never forget it.

Within days, things began to turn around. I was asked to appear on several television shows to promote my book. I was asked to be a guest on The Shopping Channel in Canada, and my appearance was very successful and very validating. People who called in kept telling me how the "Attacking Anxiety and Depression" program had saved their life and how they believed God had sent them to us. It was so empowering. The business took off and has been thriving ever since.

Making Miracles Happen

Do I believe in miracles? I am absolutely certain they exist. Do I think we can make them happen in our own lives and the lives of others? I know we can, and so do you.

In my experience, there are two types of miracles:

1. *Spiritually related events we can't explain.* These are the miracles that make our hearts leap with joy for the confirmation that there is life after death, that there is Someone who hears our prayers, that there is another dimension, and that anything is possible. These types of miracles happen daily, but you have to look for them and expect them.

2. *Remarkable things we can create for ourselves and others.* Helping to change lives and make a difference in the world is a miracle. But we must look for opportunities to be a miracle worker on a regular basis and make a sincere effort to do so.

It never ceases to amaze me how easy it is to perform a miracle in someone else's life. I have been blessed with the ability of giving people hope. I can help them create the miracle of recovery in their own lives when they struggle with anxiety and depression. I see the miracles we create for each other when we offer kindness, encouragement, and love. These simple things can literally change a person's life. What miracle can you give to someone? When was the last time you asked for, *prayed for,* a miracle for yourself?

Possibly you've asked for miracles before and didn't get them. Maybe you have lost loved ones or struggled with insurmountable problems in your own life when you've asked for help and didn't feel you received it. Perhaps you didn't feel anyone even heard your prayer. Don't stop now. With renewed thinking skills and your healthy new belief in yourself and the universe around you, your heart is more open than it has ever been before. Now you know how to look for and receive divine guidance. I believe you will look more often and will pay more attention to the signs.

The Power of Prayer

Prayer is a wonderful method of clarifying your desires, asking for help, and even asking for a miracle. What are the purposes of prayer?

Prayer helps us to clarify our problems. It allows us the opportunity to open up and to ask for clarification. It helps us to be honest with ourselves and to analyze the situation from a more humble, less worldly perspective.

Prayer is a means of "sharing the burden," which relieves some of the pressure. Prayer is sharing our worries and concerns with someone who will listen and won't judge us, which is something we all need. In addition, prayer hands the problem over to someone else, and sometimes that in itself is enough to relieve the burden.

Prayer allows us to talk it out. It allows us to verbalize what we are dealing with and to ask for guidance and different perspectives.

Prayer expresses sincere heartfelt energy. When we pray, we are exposing our real selves and extending sincere, loving energy. It isn't about fancy words or doing it right, it is about opening your heart and being sincere.

Prayer connects us with higher powers, enabling us to ask for and to create miracles. Prayer is our connection with God and the universe. It is, I believe, universal communication on its highest level.

Prayer is a place where we can find a spiritual wholeness that many of us have been missing. Prayer is a form of communication with ourselves, with God, and with other people. It is a time when we open ourselves up to our vulnerabilities and

show our whole selves. We understand and examine our deep-
est longings and needs. Is God in your family? Are you spiri-
tually deficient? Prayer can help.

If prayer is something that is new to you or something you aren't
sure how to do, I would like to make the following suggestions
that have worked for me:

- Acknowledge God: speak directly to him and be humble.
- Be grateful: start with all the things you are thankful for.
- Be honest: God knows it all anyway, you can't hide it from
  him.
- Don't judge yourself: no one is perfect; we all make mistakes.
- Don't wait for the perfect time: there is no perfect time.
- Pray often: say small prayers throughout the day, it will make
  you feel better.
- Pray when you're happy (not just when you want something):
  thank God for the day, for anything and everything.

There is no right or wrong way to pray. You don't have to be in a
church or on your knees. It doesn't have to be in a certain place or
at a certain time. You don't have to use specific words. You will find
that Corporate Prayer, which is more formal and is usually led by
clergy, comes from a text and is done in a group setting. But private, individual prayer doesn't have to be that complicated. I find it
is similar to meditating. You get quiet, go inside yourself, and
speak to God. Lose yourself in the prayer. Let it take you to a different place of calmness and serenity. Let it provide you with a
sense of comfort. I also believe that whenever two or more are

gathered to pray, it makes your prayer that much stronger. I have seen it happen time and time again in my own life.

Faith

Faith is an absolute belief in something. It is energy, emotion, and conviction. It is relinquishing yourself to something you trust. You determine what you want to have faith in and then you move forward with quiet confidence. It seems the more intellectual someone is, the harder it is for that person to have faith. The more you read, study, and intellectualize, the less logical the whole idea of faith becomes. Faith isn't something you can research and intellectualize. It isn't something you have to educate yourself about to obtain. You just have to allow yourself to experience it, in spite of how simple it sounds. That is the point after all—it is simple.

There are many people and things in my life in which I have faith. I have faith that my husband will not be unfaithful or abuse my trust. I have faith that he is my partner in life and that he is there for me. I have faith in my children. I know who they are, and I believe that they will continue to be honest and forthright and to make good decisions. I have faith in my employees. I trust them and trust their judgment and dedication. I also have tremendous faith in God and faith in the principles of right and wrong and universal law. These things give me comfort, help guide me in making decisions, and offer me support when nothing else makes sense. What do you have faith in?

I believe religion and spiritual beliefs are a personal thing. Let's face it, none of us knows for sure what is really out there or up there. No one knows for sure what is absolute truth. Unless you've died and come back again, you can only go on what you've been taught and what you've studied. It is your personal journey. I think it would be difficult to get through the rough times or even fully appreciate the good times without faith.

So many times in my personal and professional life, my faith in the belief that I was on the right side of the force, so to speak, that I was doing good things and going in the right direction, kept me persisting through the difficult times. I could not have made it this far without my faith—faith in God, faith in myself and my mission, faith in my talent, faith that doing the right thing would eventually get me where I wanted to go, faith that things were going the way they should in spite of how it looked on the outside.

Faith is a calm resolution that things will work out, one way or another. Faith is belief without proof. It is "just knowing." It is uncomplicated, because when it becomes complicated and conditional, it is no longer faith.

Do you have faith in yourself, in others, in God? If you aren't sure, I suggest you start to find the answers through prayer. Ask for the power to begin to have faith. Begin to relax and to let go of some of your concerns, and trust that you aren't alone. The more you begin to relinquish some of your need to control, your need to have everything be logical, the more you let yourself relax and trust faith, the more faith becomes natural to you.

The Importance of a Spiritual Connection

Whether you are Christian, Jewish, or Muslim, individual suffering in the world is widely and sadly apparent, and it isn't religion specific or prejudice. It manifests in all of us in the form of unhappiness, anger, depression, guilt, jealousy, illness, and disease. To cope with all this turmoil and still stay motivated and passionate about life, we need to have something in which to believe.

The positive energy forces of the universe are yours to call on whenever you want them. But you have to believe they exist and know how to use them. It all begins with you. You are your own source of abundance. Think of your thoughts as magnets. Your thinking must be clear, distinct, and sharply defined. It must stay positive and focused. When you focus, you have the power to bring the things you desire to your life. Your focused thoughts elicit emotions; your emotions energize your actions. The stronger your emotions are, the more likely you are to take action and the more action you're likely to take. Faith will help you to maintain your focus on exactly what it is you do want, and it will keep you moving toward your goal until you achieve it.

Don't waste any more time with negative, destructive thinking and behavior. Don't use up all your energy with worry and fear. Instead, wallow in the miracle that life is, that you are.

> *Do you realize what this means?*
> *The fact of being alive . . .*
> *I still find it staggering that I am here at all.*
> —CHRISTOPHER LEACH

EPILOGUE

For God hath not given us the Spirit of fear;
but of Power,
of Love,
and of sound mind.

— TIMOTHY 1 : 17

People are inclined to act or react out of fear rather than out of a desire for personal growth. Few of us take on a serious challenge or choose an unfamiliar path as a result of an overwhelming desire to explore the new and to improve ourselves. Most personal changes and challenges, experiences that can eventually bring us tremendous growth and insight, are the result of pain and turmoil with which we are forced to deal. Many people stay stuck in a self-limited, risk-avoiding way of living, one that bypasses difficulties—willing to live with the familiar, no matter how colorless the rewards, to avoid the anxiety that often accompanies the unfamiliar.

Many of us complain, insisting that what we need is change, but deep down our true desire is to remain in our comfort zone and still get what we want, without taking risks. But facing our fears and taking risks is the only way to a truly limitless life.

So what do we all want? Is there a general definition of success and personal satisfaction that would apply to us all? There certainly are desires we all share. We want to enjoy our lives, our careers, and our relationships. We want to love and be loved. We want to be and feel healthy. We want to feel needed, important, and appreciated. We want to feel that our lives have value. We want to be financially secure and independent. We want to feel attractive and confident. We want to get up feeling good about the day ahead of us and go to bed at night feeling contented and peaceful. We want to feel that we have control of our lives. We want a sense of contentment.

You were meant to be happy, to prosper, and to live a good life. You were meant to be peaceful and satisfied. In this book, the operative principle is acknowledging that you already have everything you need to be truly successful and satisfied. You are unique, talented, smart, and creative. You are capable of great things and deserving of a good life. Opportunity is ongoing and endless. Abundance awaits you. You just need clarity, motivation, and faith, and you need to reestablish your power.

The time has come. No more excuses. You must know what you want and be on a clear path to get it. By clarifying your dreams and devising a solid plan of action, by acquiring an attitude of success, achievement, maturity, and empowerment, and by working with universal energy and intuitive principles, a transformational process will occur. You will change; therefore your life will change. You will put forth a higher, more positive energy, and a synergy will be created. You will command positive energy and draw it to you. Positive experiences will come your way. Interesting, uplifting people will be drawn to you. And your life will become a wonderful and exciting journey, bringing you more abundance and fulfillment than you ever thought possible.

Life is the most precious gift of all. You are, at this very moment, making choices that will affect how you live, how happy you are, what the future holds for you, and what you will look back on in the form of a lifetime of memories. Will you be grateful? Will you feel satisfied? Choose carefully, my friend.

I challenge you to embrace this new approach. Make the conscious choice to live the life you desire. Look squarely at the fear that is associated with risk and challenge and embrace it, for it brings with it a bounty of self-esteem and tremendous potential for living a life without limits. I hope you will go forward with the grace of God, a newfound clarity, and absolute faith that anything and everything is awaiting you.

FROM PANIC
TO POWER

READ BY THE AUTHOR
LUCINDA BASSETT

A combination of Lucinda Bassett's personal story
and her program, containing techniques and skills that
the program teaches, as well as case histories and
testimonials from participants.

ISBN 0-694-51595-7
$16.00 ($21.50 Can.)
2 Hours • 2 Cassettes
ABRIDGED

Available wherever books are sold, or call 1-800-331-3761 to order.

HarperAudio
An Imprint of HarperCollins*Publishers*
www.harperaudio.com

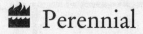
Perennial

Also by Lucinda Bassett:

FROM PANIC TO POWER
Proven Techniques to Calm Your Anxieties,
Conquer Your Fears, and Put You in Control

A transforming journey from fear,
anxiety, and panic to success, personal
power, and peace of mind. Lucinda
Bassett developed the internationally
acclaimed Attacking Anxiety program—
a combination of techniques and skills
that helps people suffering from anxiety
and panic attacks to overcome their
fears and regain their independence.
Her powerful program, which teaches
people how to think differently and
respond in a less anxious way, has
already enabled thousands all over
the world to transform their draining
doubts, fears, and anxieties into
powerful, positive energy and
newfound freedom.

ISBN 0-06-092758-5 (paperback)